Kiekelly

TOUCHING PEACE

Books by Thich Nhat Hanh

Being Peace

Breathe! You Are Alive:
Sutra on the Full Awareness of Breathing

The Diamond that Cuts through Illusion:
Commentaries on the Prajñaparamita Diamond Sutra

A Guide to Walking Meditation

The Heart of Understanding:
Commentaries on the Prajñaparamita Heart Sutra

Interbeing: Commentaries on the Tiep Hien Precepts

The Miracle of Mindfulness: A Manual on Meditation

The Moon Bamboo

Old Path White Clouds:
Walking in the Footsteps of the Buddha

Our Appointment with Life:
Buddha's Teaching on Living in the Present

Peace Is Every Step:
The Path of Mindfulness in Everyday Life

The Pine Gate

Present Moment Wonderful Moment:
Mindfulness Verses for Daily Living

A Rose for Your Pocket

The Sun My Heart:
From Mindfulness to Insight Meditation

The Sutra on the Eight Realizations of the Great Beings

Transformation and Healing:
Sutra on the Four Establishments of Mindfulness

Zen Poems

TOUCHING PEACE
Practicing the Art of Mindful Living

THICH NHAT HANH

Edited by Arnold Kotler
Drawings by Mayumi Oda

Parallax Press
Berkeley, California

Parallax Press
P.O. Box 7355
Berkeley, California 94707

Cover design by Gay Reineck. Text design by Ayelet Maida, based on the design of *Being Peace*. Back cover photograph by Karen Hagen Liste. Front cover image designed by Andrew Cooper and Lawrence Watson as the logo of the Buddhist Peace Fellowship, Box 4650, Berkeley, CA 94704. Special thanks to Mr. Laurance S. Rockefeller for making this publication possible. Thanks to Carol Melkonian, Shonen Bressler, and Allesandra Cornero for transcribing the tapes; to Brother David Steindl-Rast, Therese Fitzgerald, Stephen Batchelor, and Mushim Ikeda for helpful insights and suggestions; to Edward M. Hays for the idea of "Today's Day" from his book *Twelve and One-Half Keys* (Forest of Peace Books, Easton, KS 66020); and to the entire Plum Village community for their support during the final editing of this book.

Library of Congress Cataloging-in-Publication Data

Nhât Hanh, Thích.
Touching peace : practicing the art of mindful living / Thich Nhat Hanh :
illustrations by Mayumi Oda.
     p. cm.
ISBN 0-938077-57-0 (pbk.) : $9.50
1. Religious life—Buddhism. I. Oda, Mayumi, 1941-
II. Title.
BQ5410.N465 1992
294.3'444—dc20   92-33718
                                             CIP

Contents

CHAPTER ONE
Life Is a Miracle 1

CHAPTER TWO
We Are All Flowers 11

CHAPTER THREE
Transforming Our Compost 23

CHAPTER FOUR
We Have Arrived 35

CHAPTER FIVE
The Happiness of One Person 47

CHAPTER SIX
Peace Treaty 61

CHAPTER SEVEN
Love in Action 73

CHAPTER EIGHT
Diet for a Mindful Society 81

CHAPTER NINE
Sangha Building 99

CHAPTER TEN
Touching Ultimate Reality 117

Resources for the Practice 130

Life Is a Miracle

*I*n Vietnam when I was a young monk, each village temple had a big bell, like those in Christian churches in Europe and America. Whenever the bell was invited to sound, all the villagers would stop what they were doing and pause for a few moments to breathe in and out in mindfulness. At Plum Village, the community where I live in France, we do the same. Every time we hear the bell, we go back to ourselves and enjoy our breathing. When we breathe in, we say, silently, "Listen, listen," and when we breathe out, we say, "This wonderful sound brings me back to my true home."

Our true home is in the present moment. To live in the present moment is a miracle. The miracle is not to walk on water. The miracle is to walk on the green Earth in the present moment, to appreciate the peace and beauty that are available now. Peace is all around us—in the world and in nature—and within us—in our bodies and our spirits. Once we learn to touch this peace, we will be healed and transformed. It is not a matter of faith; it is a matter of practice. We need only to find ways to bring our body and mind back to the present moment so we can touch what is refreshing, healing, and wondrous.

Last year in New York City, I rode in a taxi, and I saw that the driver was not at all happy. He was not in the present moment. There was no peace or joy in him, no capacity of being alive while doing the work of driving, and he expressed it in the way he drove. Many of us do the same. We rush about, but we are not at one with what we are doing; we are not at peace. Our body is here, but our mind is somewhere else—in the past or the future, possessed by anger, frustration, hopes, or dreams. We are not really alive; we are like ghosts. If our beautiful child were to come up to us and offer us a smile, we would miss him completely, and he would miss us. What a pity!

In *The Stranger*, Albert Camus described a man who was going to be executed in a few days. Sitting alone in his cell, he noticed a small patch of blue sky through the skylight, and suddenly he felt deeply in touch with life, deeply in the present moment. He vowed to live his remaining days in mindfulness, in full appreciation of each moment, and he did so for several days. Then, just three hours before the time of his execution, a priest came into the cell to receive a confession and administer the last rites. But the man wanted only to be alone. He tried many ways to get the priest to leave, and when he finally succeeded, he said to himself that that priest lived like a dead man.

"Il vit comme un mort." He saw that the one who was trying to save him was less alive than he, the one who was about to be executed.

Many of us, although alive, are not really alive, because we are not able to touch life in the present moment. We are like dead people, as Camus says. I would like to share with you a few simple exercises we can practice that can help us reunify our body and mind and get back in touch with life in the present moment. The first is called conscious breathing, and human beings like us have been practicing this for more than three thousand years. As we breathe in, we know we are breathing in, and as we breathe out, we know we are breathing out. As we do this, we observe many elements of happiness inside us and around us. We can really enjoy touching our breathing and our being alive.

Life is found only in the present moment. I think we should have a holiday to celebrate this fact. We have holidays for so many important occasions— Christmas, New Year's, Mother's Day, Father's Day, even Earth Day—why not celebrate a day when we can live happily in the present moment all day long. I would like to declare today "Today's Day," a day dedicated to touching the Earth, touching the sky, touching the trees, and touching the peace that is available in the present moment.

Ten years ago, I planted three beautiful Himalayan cedars outside my hermitage, and now, whenever I walk by one of them, I bow, touch its bark with my cheek, and hug it. As I breathe in and out mindfully, I look up at its branches and beautiful leaves. I receive a lot of peace and sustenance from hugging trees. Touching a tree gives both you and the tree great pleasure. Trees are beautiful, refreshing, and solid. When you want to hug a tree, it will never refuse. You can rely on trees. I have even taught my students the practice of tree-hugging.

At Plum Village, we have a beautiful linden tree that provides shade and joy to hundreds of people every summer. A few years ago during a big storm, many of its branches were broken off, and the tree almost died. When I saw the linden tree after the storm, I wanted to cry. I felt the need to touch it, but I did not get much pleasure from that touching. I saw that the tree was suffering, and I resolved to find ways to help it. Fortunately, our friend Scott Mayer is a doctor for trees, and he took such good care of the linden tree that now it is even stronger and more beautiful than before. Plum Village would not be the same without that tree. Whenever I can, I touch its bark and feel it deeply.

In the same way that we touch trees, we can touch ourselves and others, with compassion. Sometimes, when we try to hammer a nail into a piece of wood, instead of pounding the nail, we pound our finger. Right away we put down the hammer and take care of our wounded finger. We do everything possible to help it, giving first aid and also compassion and concern. We may need a doctor or nurse to help, but we also need compassion and joy for the wound to heal quickly. Whenever we have some pain, it is wonderful to touch it with compassion. Even if the pain is inside—in our liver, our heart, or our lungs—we can touch it with mindfulness.

Our right hand has touched our left hand many times, but it may not have done so with compassion. Let us practice together. Breathing in and out three times, touch your left hand with your right hand and, at the same time, with your compassion. Do you notice that while your left hand is receiving comfort and love, your right hand is also receiving comfort and love? This practice is for both parties, not just one. When we see someone suffering, if we touch her with compassion, she will receive our comfort and love, and we will also receive comfort and love. We can do the same when we ourselves are suffering. Touching in this way, everyone benefits.

The best way to touch is with mindfulness. You know, it is possible to touch without mindfulness. When you wash your face in the morning, you might touch your eyes without being aware that you are touching them. You might be thinking about other things. But if you wash your face in mindfulness, aware that you have eyes that can see, that the water comes from distant sources to make washing your face possible, your washing will be much deeper. As you touch your eyes, you can say, "Breathing in, I am aware of my eyes. Breathing out, I smile to my eyes."

Our eyes are refreshing, healing, and peaceful elements that are available to us. We pay so much attention to what is wrong, why not notice what is wonderful and refreshing? We rarely take the time to appreciate our eyes. When we touch our eyes with our hands and our mindfulness, we notice that our eyes are precious jewels that are fundamental for our happiness. Those who have lost their sight feel that if they could see as well as we do, they would be in paradise. We only need to open our eyes, and we see every kind of form and color—the blue sky, the beautiful hills, the trees, the clouds, the rivers, the children, the butterflies. Just sitting here and enjoying these colors and shapes, we can be extremely happy. Seeing is a miracle, a condition for our happiness, yet most of the time we take it for granted. We don't act as if we are in paradise. When we practice breathing in and becoming aware of our eyes, breathing out and smiling to our eyes, we touch real peace and joy.

We can do the same with our heart. "Breathing in, I am aware of my heart. Breathing out, I smile to my heart." If we practice this a few times, we will realize that our heart has been working hard, day and night, for many years to keep us alive. Our heart pumps thousands of gallons of blood every day, without stopping. Even while we sleep, our heart continues its work to bring us peace and well-being. Our heart is an element of peace and joy, but we don't touch or appreciate it. We only touch the things that make us suffer, and because of that, we give our heart a hard time by our worries and strong emotions, and by what we eat and drink. Doing so, we undermine our own peace and joy. When we practice breathing in and becoming aware of our heart, breathing out and smiling to our heart, we become enlightened. We see our heart so clearly. When we smile to our heart, we are massaging it with our compassion. When we know what to eat and what not to eat, what to drink and what not to drink, what worries and despair we should avoid, we will keep our heart safe.

The same practice can be applied to other organs in our body, for instance our liver. "Breathing in, I know that my liver has been working hard to keep me well. Breathing out, I vow not to harm my liver by drinking too much alcohol." This is love meditation. Our eyes are us. Our heart is us. Our liver is us. If we cannot love our own heart and our own liver, how can we love another person? To practice love is, first of all, to practice love directed toward ourselves—taking care of our body, taking care of our heart, taking care of our liver. We are touching ourselves with love and compassion.

When we have a toothache, we know that not having a toothache is a wonderful thing. "Breathing in, I am aware of my non-toothache. Breathing out, I smile at my non-toothache." We can touch our non-toothache with our mindfulness, and even with our hands. When we have asthma and can hardly breathe, we realize that breathing freely is a wonderful thing. Even when we have just a stuffed nose, we know that breathing freely is a wonderful thing.

Every day we touch what is wrong, and, as a result, we are becoming less and less healthy. That is why we have to learn to practice touching what is not wrong—inside us and around us. When we get in touch with our eyes, our heart, our liver, our breathing, and our non-toothache and really enjoy them, we see that the conditions for peace and happiness are already present. When we walk mindfully and touch the Earth with our feet, when we drink tea with friends and touch the tea and our friendship, we get healed, and we can bring this healing to society. The more we have suffered in the past, the stronger a healer we can become. We can learn to transform our suffering into the kind of insight that will help our friends and society.

We do not have to die to enter the Kingdom of Heaven. In fact we have to be fully alive. When we breathe in and out and hug a beautiful tree, we are in Heaven. When we take one conscious breath, aware of our eyes, our heart, our liver, and our non-toothache, we are transported to Paradise right away. Peace is available. We only have to touch it. When we are truly alive, we can see that the tree is part of Heaven, and we are also part of Heaven. The whole universe is conspiring to reveal this to us, but we are so out of touch that we invest our resources in cutting down the trees. If we want to enter Heaven on Earth, we need only one conscious step and one conscious breath. When we touch peace, everything becomes real. We become ourselves, fully alive in the present moment, and the tree, our child, and everything else reveal themselves to us in their full splendor.

"The miracle is to walk on Earth." This statement was made by Zen Master Lin Chi. The miracle is not to walk on thin air or water, but to walk on Earth.

The Earth is so beautiful. We are beautiful also. We can allow ourselves to walk mindfully, touching the Earth, our wonderful mother, with each step. We don't need to wish our friends, "Peace be with you." Peace is already with them. We only need to help them cultivate the habit of touching peace in each moment.

CHAPTER TWO

We Are All Flowers

*I*n the Zen tradition, poetry and meditation always go together. Poetry is made of images and music, and images make the practice easy. Here is an exercise to help us in the practice of mindfulness that many friends have found inspiring and effective:

> Breathing in, I know I am breathing in.
> Breathing out, I know I am breathing out.
> *In/Out.*
>
> Breathing in, I see myself as a flower.
> Breathing out, I feel fresh.
> *Flower/Fresh.*
>
> Breathing in, I see myself as a mountain.
> Breathing out, I feel solid.
> *Mountain/Solid.*

Breathing in, I see myself as still water.
Breathing out, I reflect things as they are.
Water/Reflecting.

Breathing in, I see myself as space.
Breathing out, I feel free.
Space/Free.

All of us, children and adults, are beautiful flowers. Our eyelids are exactly like rose petals, especially
when our eyes are closed. Our ears are like morning
glories listening to the sounds of the birds. Our lips
form a beautiful flower every time we smile. And our
two hands are a lotus flower with five petals. The
practice is to keep our "flowerness" alive and
present, not just for our own benefit but for the happiness of everyone.

You know that if you leave a flower out of water
for several hours, the stem will dry out. When you
put it back, it may be too late; it may not be able to
absorb the water. To save the flower, you have to cut
the stem again, if possible while it is submerged so
the water can flow into the cells right away. You can
even cut the sides of the stem a little, to help the water flow in laterally. Within a short time, your flower
will bloom again.

Each of us is a flower, but sometimes our flowerness is tired and needs to be revived. We human
flowers need air. If we breathe in and out deeply and
consciously, we will bloom right away. We can
breathe while sitting, standing, lying down, or walk-

ing and, after just a few minutes, we will be fresh
enough to share our flowerness with others. Our
friends need us to be a flower. When they are sad, if
they see us looking happy, they will remember to return to their own flowerness and smile again. We
support each other. If we know how to revive our
flowerness when it is not very fresh, we provide a
real community service.

Meditation is to bring peace, joy, and harmony to
ourselves and others. "Stopping" is the basic practice
of meditation. To keep our flowerness fresh, we have
to learn how to stop our worries, anxieties, agitation,
and sadness so that we can find peace and happiness,
and smile again. When things are not going well, it is
good to stop in order to prevent the unpleasant, destructive energies from continuing. Stopping does
not mean repressing; it means, first of all, calming. If
we want the ocean to be calm, we don't throw away
its water. Without the water, nothing is left. When we
notice the presence of anger, fear, and agitation in us,
we don't need to throw them away. We only have to
breathe in and out consciously, and that alone is
enough to calm the storm. We do not need to wait for
a storm to begin to practice. When we are not suffering, conscious breathing will make us feel wonderful,
and it is the best way to prepare ourselves to deal
with troubles when they come.

Breathing is the best way to stop—to stop unhappiness, agitation, fear, and anger. You can practice
while sitting, lying down, walking, standing, or in
any position. It is especially pleasant to practice out-

doors, where the air is so refreshing. You can lie down or sit on the grass or walk slowly and breathe in and out, focusing your attention on each breath. Without thinking of anything else, you say, silently, *"Breathing in, I know I am breathing in. Breathing out, I know I am breathing out."* If you want, you can just say *"In"* as you breathe in, and *"Out"* as you breathe out. We know that those who have asthma only want to breathe freely, and we remember how enjoyable breathing can be. Breathing nourishes us, and it can bring us a lot of happiness. Please practice "In/Out" as many times as you wish—five times, ten times, twenty times, or more. It is essential for the practice of stopping, calming, and returning to our true home in the present moment.

Then, when you feel ready, try the second verse, *"Breathing in, I see myself as a flower. Breathing out, I feel fresh."* When you breathe in, say *"Flower"* and when you breathe out, say *"Fresh."* Even though we were born as flowers, after a lifetime of worries and anxiety, we may not be fresh anymore. We may have not taken good enough care of our flowerness. Practicing this verse, we water our flower. If we do it well, every cell in our body will smile, and in just five or ten seconds, the time it takes to breathe in and out, we will restore our flowerness. We continue until our flowerness becomes solid.

When we see someone who is very fresh, we like to sit close to him. He knows how to preserve himself as a flower. With mindful breathing, we can also be fresh. Young people who have not suffered much are still beautiful flowers, the kind of flowers that can be a source of joy for anyone at any time. Just by breathing in and out and smiling, we too have a flower to offer, and the more we practice breathing and smiling, the more beautiful our flower will become. A flower does not have to do anything to be of service, it only has to be a flower. That is enough. A human being, if she is a true human being, is enough to make the whole world rejoice. So please practice breathing in and out and recover your flowerness. You do it for all of us. Your freshness and your joy bring us peace.

"Breathing in, I see myself as a mountain. Breathing out, I feel solid. Mountain/Solid." This is best practiced sitting on a cushion on the floor, if possible in the lotus or half-lotus position. These are very stable positions, and the stability of your body helps bring about the stability of your mind. It is helpful to choose a cushion that is the right thickness to support you. To sit in the lotus position, place one foot (for the half-lotus) or both feet (for the full-lotus) on the opposite thighs. If this is too difficult, you can sit in any comfortable position, but try to keep your back straight and your hands gently folded on your lap. If you prefer to sit in a chair, your feet should be flat on the floor and your hands on your lap. Or if you want to lie on your back, keep your legs straight and your arms at your sides.

Picture a tree in a storm. At the top of the tree, the small branches and leaves are swaying violently in the wind. The tree looks vulnerable, quite fragile—it seems it can break at any time. But if you look at the trunk, you will see that the tree is solid; and if you look down to its root structure, you will know that the tree is deeply and firmly rooted in the soil. The tree is quite strong. It can resist the storm. We are also a kind of tree. Our trunk, our center, is just below our navel. The zones of our thinking and our emotions are at the levels of our head and chest. When we are taken hold of by a strong emotion, like despair, fear, anger, or jealousy, we should do our best to leave the zone of the storm and go down to the valley to practice breathing in and out. If we stay in the winds of the storm, it may be too dangerous. We can go for refuge into the trunk, breathing in and out, aware of the rising and falling of our abdomen.

Many people do not know how to handle emotions. When a strong feeling takes hold of them, they cannot bear it, and they may even contemplate suicide. This is because they are caught in the heart of the storm, where they feel helpless. They feel that all of life is this one emotion—fear, despair, anger, or jealousy—and that the only way to end their suffering is to end their life.

We have to practice conscious breathing so that we can learn how to cope when difficult moments come and strong emotions take hold of us. "Breathing in, I see myself as a mountain. Breathing out, I feel solid. Mountain/Solid." If you are attentive to the rise and fall of your abdomen, you can help it rise a little more as you breathe in, and you can bring it in a little closer as you breathe out. Practicing like this for a few minutes, you will see that you are stronger than you thought. You are much more than your emotion. An emotion comes, stays for a while, and goes—that is its nature. Why should we die because of an emotion? It will always pass, sooner or later. Go down to the trunk and hold on to it firmly, breathing in and out. After a few minutes, your emotion will subside, and you can practice walking meditation, sitting meditation, or drinking tea in mindfulness.

Don't wait for conditions to become adverse to begin. If you practice breathing in "Mountain," breathing out "Solid" daily, it will become a habit in less than three weeks. Then, when strong emotions come up, it will be easy for you just to observe them until they pass. If you practice while lying down before going to sleep, you will go peacefully into your sleep. There is a mountain in you. Please get in touch with it. You are more solid and resilient than you think.

Meditation is not to avoid problems or run away from difficulties. We do not practice to escape. We practice to have enough strength to confront problems effectively. To do this, we must be calm, fresh, and solid. That is why we need to practice the art of stopping. When we learn to stop, we become more calm, and our mind becomes clearer, like clear water after the particles of mud have settled. Sitting quietly, just breathing in and out, we develop strength, concentration, and clarity. So sit like a mountain. No wind can blow the mountain down. If you can sit for half an hour, enjoy sitting for half an hour. If you can sit for a few minutes, enjoy sitting for a few minutes. That is already good.

"*Breathing in, I see myself as still water. Breathing out, I reflect things as they are. Water/Reflecting.*" Near the mountain, there is a lake with clear, still water reflecting the mountain and the sky with pristine clarity. You can do the same. If you are calm and still enough, you can reflect the mountain, the blue sky, and the moon exactly as they are. You reflect whatever you see exactly as it is, without distorting anything.

Have you ever seen yourself in a mirror that distorts the image? Your face is long, your eyes are huge, and your legs are really short. Don't be like that mirror. It is better to be like the still water on the mountain lake. We often do not reflect things clearly, and we suffer because of our wrong perceptions. In *Being Peace*, I used this example: Suppose you are walking in the twilight and see a snake. You scream and run into the house to get your friends, and all of you run outside with a flashlight. But when you shine your light on the snake, you discover that it isn't a snake at all, just a piece of rope. This is a distorted perception.

When we see things or listen to other people, we often don't see clearly or really listen. We see and hear our projections and our prejudices. We are not clear enough, and we have a wrong perception. Even if our friend is giving us a compliment, we may argue with him because we distort what he says. If we are not calm, if we only listen to our hopes or our an-

ger, we will not be able to receive the truth that is trying to reflect itself on our lake. We need to make our
water still if we want to receive reality as it is. If you
feel agitated, don't do or say anything. Just breathe in
and out until you are calm enough. Then ask your
friend to repeat what he has said. This will avoid a
lot of damage. Stillness is the foundation of understanding and insight. Stillness is strength.

The practice of stopping and calming contains in it
the practice of insight. Not only the mountain, but
everything—the trees, the wind, the birds, everything
inside and around us—wants to reflect itself in us.
We don't have to go anywhere to obtain the truth. We
only need to be still and things will reveal themselves
in the still water of our heart.

The refreshing moon of the Buddha
is traveling in the sky of utmost emptiness.
If the pond of the mind is still,
the beautiful moon will reflect itself in it.

*"Breathing in, I see myself as space. Breathing out, I
feel free. Space/Free."* When you arrange flowers, it is
good to leave space around each flower so it can reveal itself in its full beauty and freshness. You don't
need a lot of flowers—two or three are enough. We
human beings also need space to be happy. We practice stopping and calming in order to offer space to
ourselves, inside and outside, and also to those we
love. We need to let go of our projects, preoccupa-

tions, worries, and regrets, and create space around us. Space is freedom.

One day the Buddha was sitting with about thirty monks in a forest near the city of Vaisali. It was early afternoon and they were about to have a dharma discussion, when a farmer came along, looking very upset. He said that all twelve of his cows had run away, and he wanted to know if the Buddha or the monks had seen them. He added that he also had two acres of sesame plants that had been eaten up by insects, and he said, "Monks, I think I am going to die. I am the unhappiest person in the world."

The Buddha replied, "Sir, we have not seen your cows. Please try looking in the other direction." After the man left, the Buddha turned to his monks and said, "Friends, you are very lucky. You don't have any cows." Our practice is to let go of our cows. If we have too many cows, inside us or around us, we should let them go. Without space, there is no way we can be happy. We take care of so many things, we worry about so many things, we have so many projects, and we think they are all crucial for our happiness; but that is not correct. The more cows we release, the happier we will be.

"The refreshing moon of the Buddha is traveling in the sky of utmost emptiness" is the image of someone who has space and freedom, inside and outside. We can do everything—walking, drinking tea, talking—in a way that reclaims our liberty. We don't have to do things under pressure. We can limit ourselves to a few projects and do them with joy and serenity. We can resist being carried away by our cows. Our freedom and happiness are too important to sacrifice for the sake of these things.

We must stop destroying our body and soul for the idea of happiness in the future. We have to learn to live happily in the present moment, to touch the peace and joy that are available now. If someone were to ask us, "Has the best moment of your life arrived yet?" we may say that it will come very soon. But if we continue to live in the same way, it may never arrive. We have to transform this moment into the most wonderful moment, and we can do that by stopping—stopping running to the future, stopping worrying about the past, stopping accumulating so many cows. You are a free person; you are alive. Open your eyes and enjoy the sunshine, the beautiful sky, and the wonderful children all around you. Breathing in and out consciously helps you become your best—calm, fresh, solid, clear, and free, able to enjoy the present moment as the best moment of your life.

CHAPTER THREE

Transforming Our Compost

When we look deeply at a flower, we can see that it is made entirely of non-flower elements, like sunshine, rain, soil, compost, air, and time. If we continue to look deeply, we will also notice that the flower is on her way to becoming compost. If we don't notice this, we will be shocked when the flower begins to decompose. When we look deeply at the compost, we see that it is also on its way to becoming flowers, and we realize that flowers and compost "inter-are." They need each other. A good organic gardener does not discriminate against compost, because he knows how to transform it into marigolds, roses, and many other kinds of flowers.

When we look deeply into ourselves, we see both flowers and garbage. Each of us has anger, hatred, depression, racial discrimination, and many other kinds of garbage in us, but there is no need for us to be afraid. In the way that a gardener knows how to transform compost into flowers, we can learn the art of transforming anger, depression, and racial discrimination into love and understanding. This is the work of meditation.

According to Buddhist psychology, our consciousness is divided into two parts, like a house with two floors. On the ground floor there is a living room, and we call this "mind consciousness." Below the ground level, there is a basement, and we call this "store consciousness." In the store consciousness, everything we have ever done, experienced, or perceived is stored in the form of a seed, or a film. Our basement is an archive of every imaginable kind of film stored on a video cassette. Upstairs in the living room, we sit in a chair and watch these films as they are brought up from the basement.

Certain movies, such as *Anger*, *Fear*, or *Despair*, seem to have the ability to come up from the basement all by themselves. They open the door to the living room and pop themselves into our video cassette recorder whether we choose them or not. When that happens, we feel stuck, and we have no choice but to watch them. Fortunately, each film has a limited length, and when it is over, it returns to the basement. But each time it is viewed by us, it establishes a better position on the archive shelf, and we know it will return soon. Sometimes a stimulus from outside, like someone saying something that hurts our feelings, triggers the showing of a film on our TV screen. We spend so much of our time watching these films, and many of them are destroying us. Learning how to stop them is important for our well-being.

Traditional texts describe consciousness as a field, a plot of land where every kind of seed can be planted—seeds of suffering, happiness, joy, sorrow, fear, anger, and hope. Store consciousness is also described as a storehouse filled with all our seeds. When a seed manifests in our mind consciousness, it always returns to the storehouse stronger. The quality of our life depends on the quality of the seeds in our store consciousness.

We may be in the habit of manifesting seeds of anger, sorrow, and fear in our mind consciousness; seeds of joy, happiness, and peace may not sprout up much. To practice mindfulness means to recognize each seed as it comes up from the storehouse and to practice watering the most wholesome seeds whenever possible, to help them grow stronger. During each moment that we are aware of something peaceful and beautiful, we water seeds of peace and beauty in us, and beautiful flowers bloom in our consciousness. The length of time we water a seed determines the strength of that seed. For example, if we stand in front of a tree, breathe consciously, and enjoy it for five minutes, seeds of happiness will be watered in us for five minutes, and those seeds will grow stronger. During the same five minutes, other seeds, like fear and pain, will not be watered. We have to practice this way every day. Any seed that manifests in our mind consciousness always returns to our store consciousness stronger. If we water our wholesome seeds carefully, we can trust that our store consciousness will do the work of healing.

Our bodies have a healing power. Every time we cut our finger, we wash the wound carefully and leave the work of healing to our body. In a few hours or a day, the cut is healed. Our consciousness also has a healing power. Suppose you see someone on the street you knew twenty years ago, and you cannot remember his name. The seed of him in your memory has become quite weak, since it has not had the chance to manifest in the upper level of your consciousness in such a long time. On your way home, you look throughout your basement to find the seed of his name, but you cannot find it. Finally you get a headache from looking so hard, so you stop looking and listen to a tape or a compact disc of beautiful music. Then you enjoy a delicious dinner and get a good night's sleep. In the morning, while you are brushing your teeth, his name just pops up. "Oh yes, that's his name." This means that during the night while your mind consciousness ceased the search, the store consciousness continued to work, and in the morning it brought you the results.

Healing has many avenues. When we feel anger, distress, or despair, we only need to breathe in and out consciously and recognize the feeling of anger, distress, or despair, and then we can leave the work of healing to our consciousness. But it is not only by touching our pain that we can heal. In fact, if we are not ready to do that, touching it may only make it worse. We have to strengthen ourselves first, and the easiest way to do this is by touching joy and peace. There are many wonderful things, but because we have focused our attention on what is wrong, we have not been able to touch what is *not* wrong. If we make some effort to breathe in and out and touch what is not wrong, the healing will be easier. Many of us have so much pain that it is difficult for us to touch a flower or hold the hand of a child. But we must make some effort so that we can develop the habit of touching what is beautiful and wholesome. This is the way we can assist our store consciousness to do the work of healing. If we touch what is peaceful and healing in us and around us, we help our store consciousness do the work of transformation. We let ourselves be healed by the trees, the birds, and the beautiful children. Otherwise, we will only repeat our suffering.

One wonderful seed in our store consciousness—the seed of mindfulness—when manifested, has the capacity of being aware of what is happening in the present moment. If we take one peaceful, happy step and we know that we are taking a peaceful, happy step, mindfulness is present. Mindfulness is an important agent for our transformation and healing, but our seed of mindfulness has been buried under many layers of forgetfulness and pain for a long time. We are rarely aware that we have eyes that see clearly, a heart and a liver that function well, and a non-toothache. We live in forgetfulness, looking for happiness somewhere else, ignoring and crushing the precious elements of happiness that are already in us and around us. If we breathe in and out and see that the tree is there, alive and beautiful, the seed of our mindfulness will be watered, and it will grow stronger. When we first start to practice, our mindfulness will be weak, like a fifteen-watt light bulb. But as soon as we pay attention to our breathing, it begins to grow stronger, and after practicing like that for a few weeks, it becomes as bright as a one-hundred-watt bulb. With the light of mindfulness shining, we touch many wonderful elements within and around us, and while doing so, we water the seeds of peace, joy, and happiness in us, and at the same time, we refrain from watering the seeds of unhappiness.

When we start out, the seeds of unhappiness in us are quite strong, because we have been watering them every day. Our seeds of anger have been watered by our spouse and our children. Because they themselves suffer, they only know how to water our seeds of suffering. When those seeds of unhappiness are strong, even if we do not invite them up from the basement, they will push the door open and barge into the living room. When they enter, it is not at all pleasant. We may try to suppress them and keep them in the basement, but because we have watered them so much, they are strong enough to just show up in the upper level of our consciousness even without an invitation.

Many of us feel the need to do something all the time—listen to a walkman, watch TV, read a book or a magazine, pick up the telephone. We want to keep ourselves busy in our living room so we can avoid dealing with the worries and anxieties that are in our basement. But if we look deeply into the nature of the

guests we are inviting into the living room, we will
see that many carry the same toxins as are present in
the negative seeds we are trying so hard to avoid.
Even as we prevent these negative seeds from coming up, we are watering them and making them
stronger. Some of us even do social and environmental work to avoid looking at our real problems.

For us to be happy, we need to water the seed of
mindfulness that is in us. Mindfulness is the seed of
enlightenment, awareness, understanding, care, compassion, liberation, transformation, and healing. If we
practice mindfulness, we get in touch with the refreshing and joyful aspects of life in us and around
us, the things we are not able to touch when we live
in forgetfulness. Mindfulness makes things like our
eyes, our heart, our non-toothache, the beautiful
moon, and the trees deeper and more beautiful. If we
touch these wonderful things with mindfulness, they
will reveal their full splendor. When we touch our
pain with mindfulness, we will begin to transform it.
When a baby is crying in the living room, his mother
goes in right away to hold him tenderly in her arms.
Because mother is made of love and tenderness,
when she does that, love and tenderness penetrate
the baby and, in only a few minutes, the baby will
probably stop crying. Mindfulness is the mother who
cares for your pain every time it begins to cry.

While the pain is in the basement, you can enjoy
many refreshing and healing elements of life by producing mindfulness. Then, when the pain wants to
come upstairs, you can turn off your walkman, close

your book, open the living room door, and invite your pain to come up. You can smile to it and embrace it with your mindfulness, which has become strong. If fear, for example, wishes to come up, don't ignore it. Greet it warmly with your mindfulness. "Fear, my old friend, I recognize you." If you are afraid of your fear, it may overwhelm you. But if you invite it up calmly and smile at it in mindfulness, it will lose some of its strength. After you have practiced watering the seeds of mindfulness for a few weeks, you will be strong enough to invite your fear to come up any time, and you will be able to embrace it with your mindfulness. It may not be entirely pleasant, but with mindfulness you are safe.

If you embrace a minor pain with mindfulness, it will be transformed in a few minutes. Just breathe in and out, and smile at it. But when you have a block of pain that is stronger, more time is needed. Practice sitting and walking meditation while you embrace your pain in mindfulness, and, sooner or later, it will be transformed. If you have increased the quality of your mindfulness through the practice, the transformation will be quicker. When mindfulness embraces pain, it begins to penetrate and transform it, like sunshine penetrating a flower bud and helping it blossom. When mindfulness touches something beautiful, it reveals its beauty. When it touches something painful, it transforms and heals it.

Another way to accelerate the transformation is called looking deeply. When we look deeply at a flower, we see the non-flower elements that help it to be—the clouds, the Earth, the gardener, the soil. When we look deeply at our pain, we see that our suffering is not ours alone. Many seeds of suffering have been handed down to us by our ancestors, our parents, and our society. We have to recognize these seeds. One boy who practices at Plum Village told me this story. When he was eleven, he was very angry at his father. Every time he fell down and hurt himself, his father would get angry and shout at him. The boy vowed that when he grew up, he would be different. But a few years ago, his little sister was playing with other children and she fell off a swing and scraped her knee. It was bleeding, and the boy became very angry. He wanted to shout at her, "How stupid! Why did you do that?" But he caught himself. Because he had been practicing mindfulness, he knew how to recognize his anger as anger, and he did not act on it.

A number of adults who were present were taking good care of his sister, washing her wound and putting a bandage on it, so he walked away slowly and practiced looking deeply. Suddenly he saw that he was exactly like his father, and he realized that if he did not do something about his anger, he would transmit it to his children. It was a remarkable insight for an eleven-year-old boy. At the same time, he saw that his father may have been a victim just like him. The seeds of his father's anger might have been transmitted by his grandparents. Because of the practice of looking deeply in mindfulness, he was able to transform his anger into insight. Then he went to his father, and told him that because he now understood him, he was able to really love him.

When we are irritated and we say something unkind to our child, we water the seeds of suffering in him. When he reacts, he waters the seeds of suffering in us. Living this way escalates and strengthens the suffering. In mindfulness, calmly breathing in and out, we can practice looking deeply at the types of suffering we have in ourselves. When we do so, we also begin to understand our ancestors, our culture, and our society. The moment we see this, we can go back and serve our people with loving kindness and compassion, and without blame. Because of our insight, we are capable of practicing real peace and reconciliation. When you remove the conflict between yourself and others, you also remove the conflict within yourself. One arrow can save two birds at the same time—if you strike the branch, both birds will fly away. First, take care of yourself. Reconcile the conflicting elements within yourself by being mindful and practicing loving kindness. Then reconcile with your own people by understanding and loving them, even if they themselves lack understanding.

The seeds of suffering are always trying to emerge. If we try to suppress them, we create a lack of circulation in our psyche and we feel sick. Practicing mindfulness helps us get strong enough to open the door to our living room and let the pain come up. Every time our pain is immersed in mindfulness, it will lose some of its strength, and later, when it returns to the store consciousness, it will be weaker.

When it comes up again, if our mindfulness is there to welcome it like a mother greeting her baby, the pain will be lessened and will go back down to the basement even weaker. In this way, we create good circulation in our psyche, and we begin to feel much better. If the blood is circulating well in our body, we experience well-being. If the energy of our mental formations is circulating well between our store consciousness and mind consciousness, we also have the feeling of well-being. We do not need to be afraid of our pain if our mindfulness is there to embrace it and transform it.

Our consciousness is the totality of our seeds, the totality of our films. If the good seeds are strong, we will have more happiness. Meditation helps the seed of mindfulness grow and develop as the light within us. If we practice mindful living, we will know how to water the seeds of joy and transform the seeds of sorrow and suffering so that understanding, compassion, and loving kindness will flower in us.

We Have Arrived

One day I was sitting on a bus in India with a friend who was organizing my visit there. My friend belonged to the caste that has been discriminated against for thousands of years. I was enjoying the view out the window, when I noticed that he was quite tense. I knew he was worried about making my time enjoyable, so I said, "Please relax. I am already enjoying my visit. Everything is fine." There was really no need for him to worry. He sat back and smiled, but, in just a few moments, he was tense again. When I looked at him, I saw the struggle that has been going on for four or five thousand years, within him as a person, and with the entire caste. Now, organizing my visit, he continued to struggle. He couldn't relax for one second.

We all have the tendency to struggle in our bodies and our minds. We believe that happiness is possible only in the future. That is why the practice "I have arrived" is very important. The realization that we have already arrived, that we don't have to travel any further, that we are already here, can give us peace and joy. The conditions for our happiness are already sufficient. We only need to allow ourselves to be in the present moment, and we will be able to touch them.

Sitting on the bus, my friend still did not allow himself to be in the present moment. He was worrying about how to make me comfortable while I was already comfortable. So I suggested that he allow himself to be, but it was not easy for him, because the habit energy had been there for a long time. Even after our bus arrived at the station and we got off, my friend still could not enjoy himself. My entire visit to India went very well, and his organizing was a complete success, but I am afraid that to this day, he is still unable to relax. We are under the influence of previous generations of our ancestors and our society. The practice of stopping and looking deeply is to stop the habit energy sustained by our negative seeds. When we are able to stop, we do it for all of them, and we end the vicious circle that is called *samsara*.

We have to live in a way that liberates the ancestors and future generations who are inside of us. Joy, peace, freedom, and harmony are not individual matters. If we do not liberate our ancestors, we will be in bondage all our lives, and we will transmit that to our children and grandchildren. Now is the time to do it. To liberate them means to liberate ourselves. This is the teaching of interbeing. As long as our an-

cestors in us are still suffering, we cannot really be
happy. If we take one step mindfully, freely, happily
touching the Earth, we do it for all previous and future generations. They all arrive with us at the same
moment, and all of us find peace at the same time.

Inside each of us is a baby we have to protect.
That baby is all future generations, and the best way
to take care of her is to practice the art of mindful living. Even before our child is conceived, she is already
there. If we take care of her now, we will be ready
when the doctor tells us that she is in our womb. In
the *Avatamsaka Sutra*, there is a story about Mahamaya, the mother of the Buddha, and a young man
named Sudhana, who vowed to attain enlightenment. Mahamaya had been living a mindful, peaceful
life, and her joyful presence was a delight to everyone. When she learned she was pregnant, she was
ready. Sudhana's teacher, Manjusri Bodhisattva, had
asked him to study with others in order to develop
his understanding, so Sudhana set off on pilgrimage.
During his travels he met fifty-three teachers, including intellectuals, workers, children, monks, nuns, lay-
persons, Buddhists, and non-Buddhists. This means
that we can learn from everyone. Among the fifty-
three was Mahamaya.

Sudhana discovered that it is not easy to get an
appointment with the mother of the Buddha. He was
advised to meditate in deep concentration if he really
wanted to see her. So he sat down, crossed his legs,
and practiced conscious breathing, and, suddenly, a
huge lotus flower with one hundred million petals

sprang forth from the Earth right in front of him. In a flash, he found himself sitting on one of the petals, which was also a huge lotus flower with one hundred million petals. Directly in front of him was Mahamaya. She was sitting on another lotus with one hundred million petals, and the petal she was sitting on was also, in itself, a huge lotus with one hundred million petals. Sudhana smiled with joy as he bowed to the mother of the Buddha.

Mahamaya could see in Sudhana that he was seeking enlightenment, and she said to him, "My deepest congratulations, young man. I am delighted to see you. I am the mother of all the buddhas in the cosmos—past, present, and future." Then she told him, "Young man, when I became pregnant with Siddhartha, the Buddha Shakyamuni, hundreds of millions of buddhas and bodhisattvas from every quarter of the universe came to pay their respects to my son. I could not refuse, and all of them entered my womb at the same time. And you know, there was more than enough room for all of them!"

At that moment, Sudhana vowed to realize enlightenment so he could wake up all living beings, and, immediately, he felt all the buddhas in the universe reaching out their arms to pat him on the head in congratulation, and their hands did not collide! When someone vows to be a bodhisattva, the effect can be felt throughout the universe. This vow is enough to change the world, and all the buddhas know this, so they pat you on the head and smile in congratulation.

In the same sutra, we read that when Diamond
Matrix attained the highest of the ten stages of a
bodhisattva, he gave a discourse about his experience
in the practice. Many other bodhisattvas came to hear
him, and after the talk, millions more bodhisattvas
named Diamond Matrix appeared from all quarters
of the universe and told him, "Congratulations! We
are also named Diamond Matrix, and we have been
giving the exact same discourse throughout the universe."

These images illustrate the principle of interbeing—the one is the many, and the many are the one.
To take good care of your baby is to take good care of
everything. In the *Avatamsaka Sutra*, the *dharmadhatu* is described as a world of light and interbeing.
The moon is in me. My beloved is in me. Those who
make me suffer are also in me. Our world of discrimination and misery is called the *lokadhatu*. It is a
world where things exist outside of each other—I am
outside of you, and Saddam Hussein is outside of
George Bush. But in the dharmadhatu, President
Hussein is in President Bush, and there is no hatred
or blaming. In the dharmadhatu, we are in the won-
der of interbeing. Life and death inter-are. No one is
afraid to die, because dying means being born as
something else at the same time. When a cloud dies,
it becomes rain. To nourish ourselves, we have to
step into the dharmadhatu.

In fact, the dharmadhatu is not different from the
lokadhatu. With one mindful step, touching the Earth
in full awareness, we enter the dharmadhatu and are

surrounded by light. We are everything else, there is
no discrimination. Everything we do for ourselves is
for others, everything we do for others is for us. Practicing mindfulness is to take the best care of the baby
in our womb and to give birth to that baby in every
moment of our life. Every moment we are awake, a
baby buddha is born. When we practice peace and
are able to smile, our peace can influence the whole
universe. Each of us is pregnant with a buddha in us.
Everyone has buddha-nature. Everyone is a buddha-
to-be. We have to take good care of our baby buddha.

After he grew up and had been practicing meditation for a number of years, looking deeply into his
body, feelings, perceptions, mental formations, and
consciousness, one day Siddhartha, the buddha-to-
be, felt that he was about to have a breakthrough.
Meditating under a beautiful pippala tree, he had the
sense that some time that night he would realize full
enlightenment and become a buddha. Suddenly,
Mara appeared. Mara sometimes appears as doubt,
sometimes as anger, darkness, jealousy, craving, or
despair. When we feel doubtful or skeptical, he is
there. When we feel angry, irritated, or lacking in
self-confidence, that is Mara. Siddhartha had been
visited by Mara many times before, and he knew that
the best way to treat him was to be very gentle.

That day Mara came in the form of skepticism. He
said, "Who do you think you are? You think you can
attain great enlightenment? Don't you realize how
much darkness, despair, and confusion there are in
the world? How can you hope to dissipate all of it?"

Siddhartha smiled, expressing great confidence. Mara continued, "I know you have practiced, but have you practiced enough? Who will witness that you have practiced long and hard enough? Who will testify that you can gain enlightenment?" Mara demanded that someone confirm that Siddhartha was going to become a buddha, a fully awakened person. At that moment, Siddhartha touched the Earth with his right hand, very deeply, with all his mindfulness, and said, "The Earth will testify for me." Suddenly, the Earth trembled and appeared as a goddess, offering him flowers, leaves, fruits, and perfumes. After that, Earth looked directly at Mara, and Mara just disappeared.

Even after the Buddha attained enlightenment, Mara continued to visit him. One time, after he had been teaching for a year and a half, he returned to his home town, Kapilavastu, to share his insight with his own family and people. One day, sitting alone, he was absorbed in the thought that there must be a nonviolent way to run a country that would avoid the kinds of suffering brought about by prisons, tortures, executions, and war and bring real happiness to people. Suddenly Mara appeared and said, "Lord Buddha, why don't you become a politician? You can apply your wisdom, knowledge, and skills as a politician." The Buddha looked directly at Mara and smiled, "Mara, my old friend, I know you well," and Mara just disappeared. The Buddha did not want to be a politician. He only wanted to be a monk, and he knew that it was Mara who was trying to tempt him to become a politician. All he did was recognize Mara and smile at him. When we recognize Mara as Mara, everything is all right.

At times we ourselves touch the Earth, but not deeply enough. When the Buddha touched the Earth with his hand, he touched it with all his mindfulness. At Plum Village, when we are visited by Mara— when we feel irritated, lacking in self-confidence, angry, or unhappy—we practice walking meditation, touching the Earth deeply with our feet. When we do it mindfully and joyfully, Mara leaves us in less than an hour.

The Earth, our mother, has brought us to life many times, and each time she receives us back into her arms. She knows everything about us, and that is why the Buddha invoked her as a witness. She appeared as a goddess, offering flowers, leaves, fruits, and perfumes to the Buddha. Then she just looked at Mara and smiled, and Mara disappeared. Mara is not much in the presence of the Earth. Every time you are approached by Mara, if you come to the Earth and ask for help by touching her deeply, the way the Buddha did, you will be offered flowers, fruits, butterflies, and many other gifts of nature, and the Earth will look at Mara in such a way that he will disappear.

We have so many reasons to be happy. The Earth is filled with love for us, and patience. Whenever she sees us suffering, she will protect us. With the Earth as a refuge, we need not be afraid of anything, even dying. Walking mindfully on the Earth, we are nourished by the trees, the bushes, the flowers, and the sunshine. Touching the Earth is a very deep practice that can restore our peace and our joy. We are children of the Earth. We rely on the Earth, and the Earth relies on us. Whether the Earth is beautiful, fresh, and green, or arid and parched, depends on our way of walking. Please touch the Earth in mindfulness, with joy and concentration. The Earth will heal you, and you will heal the Earth.

One of the best ways to touch the Earth is by practicing walking meditation. We walk slowly, massaging the Earth and planting seeds of joy and happiness with each step, and following our breathing at the same time. We don't try to go anywhere. We arrive with every step. When we breathe in, we count the number of steps we take. If we take three steps, we say, silently, "In, in, in." When we breathe out, we do the same, "Out, out, out." If we take three steps as we breathe in and four steps as we breathe out, we say "Out, out, out, out." We listen to the needs of our lungs, and we breathe and walk accordingly. Walking up a hill, we will probably take fewer steps with each breath. As we walk, we bring our attention down into our feet. We breathe as if we were breathing from the soles of our feet. We don't stay in the zone of our thoughts and emotions.

After practicing "In, in, in," and "Out, out, out," five or ten times, you might like to practice "Flower, flower, flower," while breathing in, and "Fresh, fresh, fresh," while breathing out. You get flowerness and freshness from the Earth and from the air. You can hold the hand of a child as you walk. The child will receive your concentration and stability, and you will receive his or her innocence and freshness. At Plum Village, I proposed to the young people a simple *gatha* for walking meditation. I wanted them to respond to life, to society, to the Earth in a positive way, so I suggested they say, "*Oui, oui, oui*," when they breathe in, and, "*Merci, merci, merci*," when they breathe out. The children liked it very much.

After practicing "Flower/Fresh," you can switch to "Mountain/Solid." Practice each exercise as many times as you wish, enjoying your walking and not arriving anywhere, except the present moment. You can practice walking meditation between business meetings, walking from your car to the market, or on any other occasion. Allow enough time to walk. Instead of three minutes, give yourself eight or ten minutes. I always give myself an extra hour when I go to the airport so that I can practice walking meditation there. My friends want to keep me visiting right up to the last minute, but I always resist. I tell them that I need the time.

To strengthen the seeds of mindfulness in us, it is helpful if sometimes we practice in a park or some other beautiful, quiet place. We walk slowly, but not too slowly, as we don't want others to think we are too unusual. This is a kind of invisible practice. We can enjoy nature and our own serenity without making others uncomfortable. When we see something we want to touch with our mindfulness—the blue sky, the hills, a tree, or a bird—we just stop, but while we do so, we continue breathing in and out mindfully. If we don't continue to breathe consciously, sooner or later our thinking will settle back in, and the bird and the tree will disappear. Therefore, we always hold on to our breathing. At Plum Village, we practice walking meditation every time we go from one place to another, even for a short distance. Whenever I see someone walking mindfully, she is a bell of mindfulness for me. If I have lost my mindfulness and I see her, I return to my mindfulness right away. As a community, we can help each other a lot.

There is no need for us to struggle to arrive somewhere else. We know that our final destination is the cemetery. Why are we in a hurry to get there? Why not step in the direction of life, which is in the present moment? When we practice walking meditation for even a few days, we will will undergo a deep transformation, and we will learn how to enjoy peace in each moment of our life. We will smile, and countless bodhisattvas throughout the cosmos will smile back at us because our peace is so deep. Everything we think, feel, and do has an effect on our ancestors and all future generations and reverberates throughout the universe. Therefore, our smile helps everyone. This is the teaching of the *Avatamsaka Sutra*. To take good care of our baby, we only need to stop struggling. Peace is every step. We have already arrived.

CHAPTER FIVE

The Happiness of One Person

*T*he practice of mindfulness is the practice of love itself. To encourage mindfulness in those who are about to live with another person, I have asked my students to help me start an Institute for the Happiness of One Person. We will have a one-year program and only one course, entitled "Looking Deeply." For a year, each student will practice looking deeply into himself in order to discover all the flowers and compost that are in him, not just of his own making but from his ancestors and society. At the end of the course, each student will receive a diploma that says he or she is qualified to be married. I think it is important for all young couples to practice in this way before embarking on the journey of mutual discovery that takes place in a marriage. If they do not come to know themselves well and take the time to untie their internal knots, the first year of their marriage will be difficult.

When we enter a relationship, we feel excitement, enthusiasm, and the willingness to explore. But we do not really understand ourselves or the other person very well yet. Living together twenty-four hours a day, we look, listen, and experience many things we have not seen or imagined before. When we fell in love, we constructed a beautiful image that we projected onto our partner, and now we are a little shocked as our illusions disappear and we discover the reality. Unless we know how to practice mindfulness together, looking deeply into ourselves and our partner, we may find it difficult to sustain our love through this period.

In Buddhist psychology, the word *samyojana* refers to internal formations, fetters, or knots. When someone says something unkind to us, for example, if we do not understand why he said it and we become irritated, a knot will be tied in us. The lack of understanding is the basis for every internal knot. If we practice mindfulness, we can learn the skill of recognizing a knot the moment it is tied in us and finding ways to untie it. Internal formations need our full attention as soon as they form, while they are still loosely tied, so that the work of untying them will be easy. If we do not untie our knots when they form, they will grow tighter and stronger. It is difficult for our mind to accept that it has negative feelings like anger, fear, and regret, so it finds ways to bury these in remote areas of our consciousness. We create elaborate defense mechanisms to deny their existence, but these problematic feelings are always trying to surface.

The first step in dealing with unconscious internal formations is to try to bring them into awareness. We meditate, practicing conscious breathing to gain access to them. They might reveal themselves as images, feelings, thoughts, words, or actions. We may notice a feeling of anxiety and ask, "Why did I feel so uncomfortable when she said that?" or "Why do I keep doing that?" or "Why did I hate that character in the movie so much?" Observing ourselves closely can bring an internal formation into view. And as we shine the light of our mindfulness on it, it begins to reveal its face. We may feel some resistance to continuing to look at it, but if we have developed the capacity to sit still and observe our feelings, the source of the knot will slowly reveal itself and give us an idea how to untie it. Practicing like this, we come to know our internal formations, and we make peace with ourselves.

When we live with another person, it is important to practice this way. To protect each other's happiness, we must learn to transform the internal formations we produce together as soon as they arise. One woman told me that three days after her wedding, she received several large internal formations from her husband, and she kept them to herself for thirty years. She was afraid that if she told him, there would be a fight. How can we be happy like that, with no real communication? When we are not mindful in our daily life, we plant the seeds of suffering in the very person we love.

But when both partners are still light and not filled with too many knots, the practice is not difficult. Together we look at the misunderstanding that created the knot, and then we untie it. For example, if we hear our husband exaggerating to his friends about something he did, we may feel a knot being tied inside us in the form of some disrespect for him. But if we discuss it with him right away, the two of us can come to a clear understanding, and the knot will be untied easily.

If we practice the art of mindful living together, we can do this. We see that the other person, like us, has both flowers and compost inside, and we accept this. Our practice is to water the flowerness in her, and not bring her more garbage. We avoid blaming and arguing. When we try to grow flowers, if the flowers do not grow well, we do not blame or argue with them. We blame ourselves for not taking care of them well. Our partner is a flower. If we take care of her well, she will grow beautifully. If we take care of her poorly, she will wither. To help a flower grow well, we must understand her nature. How much water does she need? How much sunshine? We look deeply into ourselves to see our true nature, and we look into the other person to see her nature.

"Suchness" is a technical term that means true nature. Everything has its suchness; that is how we recognize it. An orange has its suchness; that is why we don't confuse it with a lemon. In my community, we cook with propane gas, and we know its suchness. We know that it can be very dangerous. If it leaks in the room while we are asleep and someone lights a match, it can kill us. But we also know that propane can help us cook a wonderful meal, and that is why we invite it into our house to live peacefully with us.

I would like to share a story about suchness. There was a patient in the mental hospital in Bien Hoa who seemed to be normal. He ate and talked like other people. But he believed that he was a kernel of corn, and every time he saw a chicken, he ran for his life. He did not know his suchness. When the nurse reported this to the doctor, the doctor told him, "Sir, you are not a kernel of corn, you are a human being. You have hair, eyes, a nose, and arms." He gave a kind of sermon like that, and finally he asked, "Now, sir, can you tell me what you are?"

The man replied, "Doctor, I am a human being. I am not a kernel of corn." The doctor was happy. He felt he had helped this patient a lot. But to be certain, he asked the man to repeat the sentence, "I am a human being, I am not a kernel of corn," four hundred times a day and to write it on a piece of paper three hundred more times each day. The man became devoted to doing it, and he stopped going out at all. He just stayed in his room repeating and writing exactly what the doctor had prescribed.

A month later, the doctor came to see him, and the nurse reported, "He is doing very well. He stays inside and practices the exercises you gave him very diligently."

The doctor asked, "Sir, how are things?"

"Very well, thank you, doctor."

"Can you tell me what you are?"

"Oh yes, doctor. I am a human being. I am not a kernel of corn."

The doctor was delighted. He said, "We will release you in a few days. Please come with me to my office." But while doctor, nurse, and patient were walking together to the office, a chicken walked by, and the man ran away so quickly that the doctor couldn't catch him. It was more than an hour later that the nurse brought him to the office.

The doctor was agitated. "You said you are a human being and not a kernel of corn. So why did you run away when you saw a chicken?"

The man said, "Of course I know that I am a human being and not a kernel of corn. But how can I be sure the chicken knows?"

Although he had been practicing very hard, he was not able to see his true nature, his suchness, and he did not understand the suchness of the chicken either. Each of us has our own suchness. If we want to live in peace and happiness with another person, we have to understand his or her suchness and our own. Once we see it, we will have no trouble living peacefully and happily together.

To meditate is to look deeply into the nature of things, including our own nature and the nature of the person in front of us. When we see the true nature of that person, we discover his or her difficulties, aspirations, suffering, and anxieties. We can sit down, hold our partner's hand, look deeply at him, and say, "Darling, do I understand you enough? Do I water your seeds of suffering? Do I water your seeds of joy? Please tell me how I can love you better." If we say this from the bottom of our heart, he may begin to cry, and that is a good sign. It means the door of communication may be opening again.

Loving speech is an important aspect of the practice. Every time the other person does something well, we should congratulate him or her to show our approval. This is especially true with children. We have to strengthen the self-esteem of our children. We have to appreciate and congratulate every good thing they say and do in order to help our children grow. We don't take things for granted. If the other person manifests some talent or capacity to love and create happiness, we must be aware of it and express our appreciation. This is the way to water the seeds of happiness. We should avoid saying destructive things like, "I doubt that you can do this." Instead, we say, "This is difficult, darling, but I have faith you can do it." This kind of talk makes the other person stronger.

When there is some problem, if we are calm enough, we can discuss it fully in a loving and nonviolent way. But if we are not calm enough, we should refrain from speaking. We can just breathe. If we need to, we can practice walking meditation in the fresh air, looking at the trees, the clouds, the river. Once we are calm and capable of using the language of loving kindness, we can talk together. If, during

our conversation, the feeling of irritation comes
up again, we can stop and just breathe. This is mindfulness.

All of us need to change and grow. When we
marry, we can make a promise to change and grow
together, sharing the fruits of our practice. When we
as a couple are happy, when understanding and harmony are there, it is easy for us to extend our happiness and joy to many people. For those who have
been married ten or twenty years, this kind of practice is also relevant. You can also enroll in our Institute and continue to develop the practice of living in
mindfulness and learning from each other. You may
think you already know everything about your
spouse, but that is not true. Physicists study one elec-
tron for many years and still do not claim to understand everything about it. How can you think you
know everything about one human being? Driving
your car, paying attention only to your thoughts, you
ignore her. If you continue to treat her that way, she
will die slowly. She needs your attention, your gar-
dening, your care.

When things become too difficult, we tend to
think of divorce. Instead, I hope you will make an effort to preserve your marriage, to return to your
spouse with more harmony and understanding.
Many people have divorced three or four times, and
they continue to make the same kinds of mistakes. If
you can take the time to open the door of communication, the door of your heart, and share your suffer-
ings and your dreams with one another, you do it not

just for yourselves but for your children and for all of us.

In Plum Village, we practice a ceremony called Beginning Anew every week. At the Institute for the Happiness of One Person, we will also practice this. During the ceremony, everyone in the community sits in a circle with a vase of fresh flowers in the center. Each of us follows our breathing as we wait for the facilitator to begin. The ceremony has three stages: flower watering, expressing regrets, and expressing hurts and difficulties. This practice helps prevent feelings of hurt from building up over the weeks and helps make the situation safe for everyone in the family or the community.

We begin with flower watering. When one person is ready to speak, she joins her palms and the others join their palms to show that she has the right to speak. Then she stands, walks slowly to the flower, takes the vase in her hands, and returns to her seat. When she speaks, her words reflect the freshness and beauty of the flower that is in her hand. During flower watering, each speaker acknowledges the wholesome, wonderful qualities of the others. It is not flattery; we always speak the truth. Everyone has some strong points that can be seen with awareness. No one can interrupt the person holding the flower. She is allowed as much time as she needs to speak, and everyone else practices deep listening. When she finishes speaking, she stands up and slowly returns the vase to the center of the room.

In the second part of the ceremony, we express our regrets for what we have done to hurt others. It does not take more than one thoughtless phrase to hurt someone. The ceremony of Beginning Anew is an opportunity for us to recall some regret from earlier in the week and undo it. In the third part of the ceremony, we express ways in which others have hurt us. Loving speech is crucial. We want to heal the community, not harm it. We speak frankly, but we do not want to be destructive. Listening meditation is an important part of the practice. When we sit among a circle of friends who are all practicing deep listening, our speech becomes more beautiful and more constructive. We never blame or argue.

Compassionate listening is crucial. We listen with the willingness to relieve the suffering of the other person, not to judge or argue with her. We listen with all our attention. Even if we hear something that is not true, we continue to listen deeply so the other person can express her pain and release the tensions within herself. If we reply to her or correct her, the practice will not bear fruit. We just listen. If we need to tell the other person that her perception was not correct, we can do that a few days later, privately and calmly. Then, at the next Beginning Anew session, she may be the person who rectifies the error and we will not have to say anything.

We close the ceremony with a song or by holding hands with everyone in the circle and breathing for a minute. Sometimes we end with hugging meditation. Afterwards we always feel light and relieved, even if

we have taken only a preliminary step towards healing. We now have confidence that, having begun, we
can continue. The practice of Beginning Anew dates
to the time of the Buddha. His communities of monks
and nuns practiced this on the eve of every full moon
and new moon.

Hugging meditation, on the other hand, is something I invented. The first time I learned hugging was
in Atlanta in 1966. A woman poet took me to the airport and then asked, "Is it all right to hug a Buddhist
monk?" In my country, we are not used to expressing
ourselves that way in public, but I thought, "I am a
Zen teacher. It should be no problem for me to do
that." So I said, "Why not?" and she hugged me, but
I was rather stiff. While on the plane, I decided that if
I wanted to work with friends in the West, I would
have to learn the culture of the West. That is why I
invented hugging meditation.

Hugging meditation is a combination of East and
West. According to the practice, you have to really
hug the person you are hugging. You have to make
him or her very real in your arms. You don't do it just
for the sake of appearance, patting him on the back
two or three times to pretend you are there. You are
really there, so you do not have to do that. You
breathe consciously while hugging, and you hug
with all your body, spirit, and heart. "Breathing in, I
know my dear one is in my arms, alive. Breathing
out, he is so precious to me." While you hold him
and breathe in and out three times, the person in
your arms becomes real, and you become very real

also. When you love someone, you want him to be happy. If he is not happy, there is no way you can be happy. Happiness is not an individual matter. True love requires deep understanding. In fact, love is another name for understanding. If you do not understand, you cannot love properly. Without understanding, your love will only cause the other person to suffer.

In Southeast Asia, many people are extremely fond of a big fruit with many thorns called durian. You might even say they are addicted to it. Its smell is extremely strong, and when some people finish eating the fruit, they put the skin under their bed so they can continue to smell it. To me, the smell of durian is horrendous.

One day when I was practicing chanting alone in my temple in Vietnam, there happened to be one durian on the altar that had been offered to the Buddha. I was trying to recite the *Lotus Sutra*, using a wooden drum and a large bowl-shaped bell for accompaniment, but I could not concentrate at all. I finally decided to turn the bell over and imprison the durian so I could chant the sutra. After I finished, I bowed to the Buddha and liberated the durian. If you were to say to me, "I love you so much I would like you to eat some of this durian," I would suffer. You love me, you want me to be happy, but you force me to eat durian. That is an example of love without understanding. Your intention is good, but you don't have the correct understanding.

In order to love properly, you have to understand. Understanding means to see the depth of the darkness, the pain, and the suffering of the other person. If you don't see that, the more you do for her, the more she will suffer. Creating happiness is an art. If during your childhood, you saw your mother or father create happiness in your family, you were able to learn from those things. But if your parents did not know how to create happiness in the family, you may not know how to do it. So in our Institute, we have to teach the art of making people happy. Living together is an art. Even with good will, you can make your partner quite unhappy. Art is the essence of life. We have to be artful in our speech and action. The substance of art is mindfulness.

When you first fall in love and you feel attached to the other person, that is not yet real love. Real love means loving kindness and compassion, the kind of love that does not have any conditions. You form a community of two in order to practice love—taking care of each other, helping your partner blossom, and making happiness something real in that small community. Through your love for each other, through learning the art of making one person happy, you learn to express your love for the whole of humanity and all beings. Please help us develop the curriculum for the Institute for the Happiness of One Person. Don't wait until we open the school. You can begin practicing right away.

Peace Treaty

*I*n Order That We May Live Long and Happily
Together, In Order That We May Continually Develop
and Deepen Our Love and Understanding, We the Un-
dersigned, Vow to Observe and Practice the Following:

I, the one who is angry, agree to:

*1. Refrain from saying or doing anything that might
cause further damage or escalate the anger.*

2. Not suppress my anger.

*3. Practice breathing and taking refuge in the island of
myself.*

*4. Calmly, within twenty-four hours, tell the one who
has made me angry about my anger and suffering, either verbally or by delivering a Peace Note.*

*5. Ask for an appointment for later in the week (e.g.
Friday evening) to discuss this matter more thoroughly,
either verbally or by Peace Note.*

6. Not say: "I am not angry. It's okay. I am not suffering. There is nothing to be angry about, at least not enough to make me angry."

7. Practice breathing and looking deeply into my daily life—while sitting, lying down, standing, and walking—in order to see:
    a. the ways I myself have been unskillful at times.
    b. how I have hurt the other person because of my own habit energy.
    c. how the strong seed of anger in me is the primary cause of my anger.
    d. how the other person's suffering, which waters the seed of my anger, is the secondary cause.
    e. how the other person is only seeking relief from his or her own suffering.
    f. that as long as the other person suffers, I cannot be truly happy.

8. Apologize immediately, without waiting until the Friday evening, as soon as I realize my unskillfulness and lack of mindfulness.

9. Postpone the Friday meeting if I do not feel calm enough to meet with the other person.

I, the one who has made the other angry, agree to:

1. Respect the other person's feelings, not ridicule him or her, and allow enough time for him or her to calm down.

2. Not press for an immediate discussion.

3. Confirm the other person's request for a meeting, either verbally or by note, and assure him or her that I will be there.

4. Practice breathing and taking refuge in the island of myself to see how:

a. I have seeds of unkindness and anger as well as the habit energy to make the other person unhappy.
b. I have mistakenly thought that making the other person suffer would relieve my own suffering.
c. by making him or her suffer, I make myself suffer.

5. Apologize as soon as I realize my unskillfulness and lack of mindfulness, without making any attempt to justify myself and without waiting until the Friday meeting.

We Vow, with Lord Buddha as Witness and the Mindful Presence of the Sangha, to Abide by These Articles and to Practice Wholeheartedly. We Invoke the Three Gems for Protection and to Grant Us Clarity and Confidence.

Signed, _____
the _____ Day of _____
in the Year _____ in _____

When we get angry, we don't look like a beautiful flower. We look more like a bomb ready to explode. Hundreds of muscles in our face tense up. Because so much suffering arises when we become angry or upset, we at Plum Village recently drafted a "Peace Treaty" which couples and individuals can sign in the presence of the sangha to increase the likelihood that we will deal with our anger well. This is not just a piece of paper; it is a practice that can help us live long and happily together. The treaty has two parts—one for the person who is angry and one for the person who has caused the anger. When we get angry or when someone is angry at us, if we follow the terms of the Peace Treaty, we will know exactly what to do and what not to do.

According to the first article, we agree that when we are angry we will refrain from saying or doing anything that might cause further damage or escalate the anger. When we know we are angry, we impose on ourselves a kind of moratorium on speech and actions.

In the second article, we agree not to suppress our anger. At the proper time, we will express something, but not immediately. The minimum waiting period is the time of three conscious breaths. If we do not wait at least that long, it may not be safe to express our feelings about our anger.

In the third article, we agree to practice breathing on our anger and taking refuge in the island of ourselves. We know that anger is there. We do not suppress it and we do not deny it. We take care of it by

producing mindfulness of breathing and embracing
it in the loving arms of mindfulness. We sit quietly or
we walk, perhaps in nature. If we need a half hour,
we take a half hour. If we need three hours, we practice breathing for three hours.

The Buddha told his students, "My friends, do not
rely on anything outside of yourselves. Be an island
unto yourself, and take refuge in the island of yourself." During difficult moments when we do not
know what to do, this is a wonderful exercise to practice. If I were in an airplane about to crash, this is
what I would practice. If we practice well, our island
will have trees, birds, a beautiful stream, and land
that is very solid. The essence of a buddha is mindfulness. Mindful breathing is the living dharma, better than any book. The sangha is present in five
elements that comprise our "self": form, feeling, perception, mental formations, consciousness. When
these elements are in harmony, we have peace and
joy. When we practice conscious breathing and produce mindfulness in ourselves, the buddha is there. If
we go back and discover the buddha within us, we
will be safe.

According to the fourth article of the treaty, we
have up to twenty-four hours to calm ourselves.
Then we must tell the other person we are angry. We
do not have the right to keep our anger any longer
than that. If we do, it becomes poisonous, and it may
destroy us and the person we love. If we are used to
the practice, we may be ready to tell him in five or
ten minutes, but the maximum is twenty-four hours.

We can say, "My dear friend, what you said this morning made me very angry. I suffered very much and I want you to know it."

According to the fifth article, we end with this sentence, "I hope that by Friday evening both of us will have had a chance to look deeply into this matter." Then we make an appointment. Friday evening is a good time to defuse all the bombs, big or small, so that we will have the whole weekend for our enjoyment. If we feel it is not yet safe for us to speak to him, if we do not feel capable of doing it in a calm way and the deadline of twenty-four hours is approaching, we can use this "Peace Note":

Date:
Time:
Dear _____,

This morning (afternoon), you said (did) something that made me very angry. I suffered very much. I want you to know this. You said (did):

Please let us both look at what you said (did) and examine the matter together in a calm and open manner this Friday evening.

Yours, not very happy right now,

If we use this note, we have to make sure the other person receives it before the deadline. We cannot just say, "I put it on your desk and you didn't look at it, so it's your fault." This is for our own good, because the moment we know that the other person has received the note, we already feel some relief. It is best to tell him directly in a calm voice, but if we think we will not be able to do it calmly, we can fill out a peace note and hand it to him. But we have to make sure he gets it before the deadline.

The sixth article tells us not to pretend we aren't angry. We may have too much pride and do not want to admit our suffering. But we shouldn't say, "I am not angry. There's nothing to be angry about." We must refrain from hiding the truth. If we are angry, that is a fact. This is an important part of the Peace Treaty. Pride should not be an obstacle that destroys our relationship. We are committed to each other, we support each other, we are a brother or sister to each other. Why should we be so proud? My pain must be his pain. My suffering must be his suffering.

According to the seventh article, while we are practicing sitting, walking, breathing, looking deeply, and living our daily life mindfully, we should focus our attention on these points: (1) Recognize the ways we have not been mindful or skillful in the past. (2) See how we have hurt the other person in the past and acknowledge to ourselves, "I have the habit energy of getting angry and hurt very easily." (3) Recognize that the main cause of our anger is the strong seed of anger in our store consciousness that has the habit of manifesting itself. The other person is not the main cause of our suffering. We have friends who do not get angry so easily. The seed of anger is in them also, but apparently their seed of anger is not as strong as ours. (4) See that the other person is suffering also, and because of this, he behaved in an unskillful way, watering the seed of anger in us. We acknowledge that he was not the main cause of our suffering. He may have been the secondary cause, or perhaps he was misperceived by us to be the secondary cause—perhaps he did not mean to hurt us at all. (5) When some people get angry, they naïvely believe that if they say something strong to another person and make him suffer, they will feel some relief. This is not a wise thing to do, but many people do it. So we have to see that the other person may only be seeking some relief from his own suffering. (6) See that as long as he continues to suffer, we cannot be truly happy. When someone in a community is unhappy, the whole community is unhappy. For us to stop suffering, we have to help the other person stop suffering. We all have to find skillful ways to help that person. Only when he overcomes his suffering will happiness in the community be authentic.

The eighth article tells us that if, during the process of looking deeply we realize our unskillfulness and lack of mindfulness, we should apologize right away. We should not make the other person feel guilty any longer. There is no need to wait until Friday evening. If we find out that we got angry because we have the habit energy of responding too

quickly or because of some misunderstanding, we
have to go to the other person and say, "I'm sorry,
I was unmindful. I got angry too easily and without
any basis. Please forgive me." He will be relieved.
It is best to stop the cycle of suffering as soon as possible.

The ninth article tells us that if, by Friday, we feel
that we are not calm enough to talk about the matter,
we should postpone the appointment for a few more
days or another week. If we are not calm, it is not yet
time to talk about it. We need to practice for a few
more days.

In the second part of the Peace Treaty, there are the
five articles concerning the one who has made the
other person angry. According to the first article,
when we see that the other person is angry, we
should respect her feelings. We shouldn't say, "I
haven't done anything, and you're angry." A feeling
has a life span—a moment to be born, some time to
stay, and then it will die down slowly. Even if we see
that her anger is not founded at all, that she is completely wrong, we don't press her to stop being angry
right away. We help her, or we leave her alone so that
her anger can die down naturally.

According to the second article, after she has told
us that she is suffering, we should not press for an
immediate discussion. If we do, everything can be
destroyed. We abide by the treaty and accept the Friday evening appointment. In the interim, we have a
chance to look deeply at the situation. "What did I
say? What did I do to make her angry?" While sit-

ting, walking, and breathing, practice looking deeply. This is true meditation.

According to the third article, after we have received a peace note, we should respond right away that we will be there on Friday evening. This is important, because if she knows we have received it, she will get some relief.

The fourth article tells us to practice breathing, taking refuge in the island of ourselves, in order to see three things: (1) We have the seeds—the habit energy—of unkindness and anger. We have made the other person unhappy before. We acknowledge that even if now we do not see our fault in her suffering. We should not be too confident that we are not responsible this time. (2) We may have been suffering, and we thought that by saying something strong to her, we would get relief. This is the wrong kind of relief, and we have to recognize that seeking that kind of relief is unwise. We shouldn't hope to suffer less by making another person suffer. (3) We look deeply and we see that her suffering is our suffering. If we do something to help her stop suffering, we will also benefit.

The fifth article tells us that if we can apologize right away, we should not wait. We can pick up the telephone and call right away, without attempting to justify or explain anything we said or did. A straightforward apology can have a powerful effect. We just say, "I am very sorry. I was not mindful or understanding." There may be no need to wait for Friday.

The Peace Treaty is a mindfulness practice. Please study it deeply and prepare carefully for the occasion to sign it. The best way to sign it is in a meditation hall, with the witness and support of the sangha. At the end of a Day of Mindfulness, in the presence of the community, you vow to abide by the articles of the treaty and practice wholeheartedly according to it. Then you sign. Unless you are committed to practicing it, it is better not to sign. If you sign and practice according to the Peace Treaty, you and your partner will benefit, and all of us will also benefit from your skill in dealing with anger.

I hope you will support the practice of the Peace Treaty by writing articles and leading retreats and discussions on the nature of the treaty and how to carry out its practice. In this way, even those who have no experience in meditation can learn and benefit from it. I believe a Peace Treaty like this will become an important part of our practice in the future. You may like to add more articles to make it more relevant to your situation. Be harmonious and happy!

Love in Action

*I*n the *Maharatnakuta Sutra*, it says that when one
bodhisattva gets angry at another bodhisattva,
countless obstacles are set up everywhere in the universe. Is it possible for a bodhisattva to get angry? Of
course it is. A bodhisattva doesn't have to be perfect.
Anyone who is aware of what is happening and tries
to wake up other people is a bodhisattva. We are all
bodhisattvas, doing our best. Along the way, we may
feel angry or frustrated from time to time. That is
why we have to practice according to the Peace
Treaty. When a bodhisattva gets angry at another
bodhisattva, countless obstacles are set up everywhere in the universe. That is understandable. We
know that when we have peace and joy in ourselves,
our peace and joy vibrate throughout the cosmos. So
when we have hatred and anger in ourselves, they
too will rebound to all quarters.

When President Bush gave the order to attack
Iraq, many of us suffered at the same time. I was at

Plum Village giving a lecture on the *Avatamsaka
Sutra*, and in the middle of a sentence, I suddenly
said, "I don't think I will go to America this spring. I
really don't want to go there now." We all paused for
a long moment to breathe, and then I resumed the
lecture. That afternoon during a tea meditation, a
number of students from North America told me that
because I felt that way, I should go. They reminded
me that friends in the U.S. had been working hard to
organize retreats there, and they helped me see that
many Americans also suffered when the President
gave the order to attack. So I decided to go in order
to support them and share their suffering.

I understood that President Bush is a bodhisattva
trying in his way to serve his people. Early in the
conflict he instituted an embargo, but because we did
not encourage him enough, he became impatient and
suddenly war was inevitable. When he ordered the
ground attack and said, "God bless the United States
of America," I knew that bodhisattva needed our
help. Any leader needs our help and our understanding. We must use intelligent and loving language so
he will listen to us. When we get angry, we cannot do
that. I listened to my American friends in Plum Village quietly and serenely, and I accepted their advice
to go to the United States.

If we get angry, countless obstacles will be set up,
blocking our way. So, without anger, we have to find
a way to tell the president that God cannot bless one
country against another. He must learn to pray better
than that. But we should not think that simply by

electing another president, the situation will be transformed. If we want a better government, we have to begin by changing our own consciousness and our own way of life. Our society is ruled by greed and violence. The way to help our country and our president is by transforming the greed and violence in ourselves and working to transform society.

Look at the 500,000 men and women from America and the West and the 1,000,000 Iraqi soldiers who spent months waiting for the land offensive to begin. They had to practice killing day and night in order to prepare. During the day, they wore helmets, took up guns and bayonets, jumped and yelled as if they were not human beings, and plunged their bayonets into sandbags representing enemy soldiers. If they did not become less than human beings, they could not have done it. They had to become inhuman to learn to kill. They did that during the day, and during the night they did the same in their dreams— planting seeds of suffering, fear, and violence within their consciousness. This is the practice of war—one and a half million men and women practicing fear and violence for many months. They knew they had to do it in order to survive.

Then the war came. The actual killing was massive, and we called it a victory. When the 500,000 troops returned home, they were deeply wounded from practicing so much violence in reality and in their consciousness. For several generations, millions of their children and grandchildren will inherit those seeds of violence and suffering. How can we call that

a victory? When the troops arrived home, they cried.
They were alive. Their families and children also
cried. Of course, they had the right to be happy, but
the men and women who returned were not the same
as the men and women who left. Their wounds will
be with us for a long time.

We have to meditate together as a nation if we
want to be able to love and understand our veterans,
our president, and our government. Eighty percent of
the American people supported the Gulf War and
called it clean and moral. They do not understand the
true nature of war. Anyone who has seen a war could
not say that. The Gulf War was not clean or moral for
the people of Iraq, or for the people of the United
States. After a war, many people, especially young
people, see violence as the way to solve problems.
The next time there is a conflict somewhere in the
world, they will be tempted to support another mili-
tary solution, another quick war. This kind of thinking and acting damages the consciousness of those
on the "winning side." If we want to protect life, we
have to look deeply as individuals and as a nation
into the true nature of war. When we see it, we have
to reveal it to the whole country by projecting it onto
a huge screen. We must learn together and do everything possible to prevent it from happening again. If
we only protest, we will not be ready when the next
war comes in five or ten years. To prevent the next
war, we have to practice peace today. If we establish
peace in our hearts and in our ways of looking at
things, war will not come. The only way to stop a

war is to have real peace. If we wait until another war is imminent to begin to practice, it will be too late.

The death of one Iraqi soldier means that one family is suffering, and more than 100,000 Iraqi soldiers and civilians were killed—we don't exactly know how many. After any war, the suffering continues on both sides for several generations. Look at the suffering of the Vietnam veterans in America and the suffering of the Vietnamese people. We have to practice mindfulness and not forget the suffering that is still going on on both sides. We need to be there for those who need us, to let them know that we share their suffering, that we suffer too. When someone feels understood, his suffering is diminished. Please don't forget this aspect of the practice.

We who have touched war have a duty to bring the truth about war to those who have not had a direct experience of it. We are the light at the tip of the candle. It is very hot, but it has the power of shining and illuminating. If we practice mindfulness, we will know how to look deeply into the nature of war, and, with our insight, wake people up so that together we can avoid repeating the same horrors again and again. We who were born from the war know what it is. The war is in us, but it is also in everyone. We all saw the video of the Los Angeles policemen beating Rodney King. When I saw those images, I identified with Rodney King, and I suffered a lot. You must have felt the same. We were all beaten at the same time. But when I looked more deeply, I saw that I am

also the five policemen. I could not separate myself
from the men who did the beating. They were manifesting the hatred and violence that pervades our
society.

Everything is ready to explode, and we are all co-
responsible. Not only does the one who is beaten suffer, but the ones who are doing the beating also suffer. If not, why would they do it? Only if you suffer
will you make other people suffer. If you are peaceful
and happy, you will not inflict suffering on other
people. The policemen also need our love and understanding. We have helped create them through our
forgetfulness, through the way we live our daily
lives. In my heart I feel no blame for anyone. Arrest-
ing and imprisoning the policemen will not help
them or solve the problem. The problem is much
deeper than that. Violence has become the substance
of our lives. The Vietnam veterans, the Persian Gulf
veterans, and the millions who absorb violence every
day are being trained to be exactly like those who did
the beating. We accept violence as a way of life, and
we water the seeds of violence in ourselves by watching violent TV programs and movies that are poisoning us and poisoning our society. If we do not transform all of this violence and misunderstanding, one
day it will be our own child who is beaten or killed,
or who is doing the beating. This is very much our
affair.

Please take the hand of your little boy or little girl
and walk slowly to the park. You may be surprised to
notice that while you are enjoying the sunshine, the

trees, and the birds, your child feels a little bored. Young people today get bored easily. They are used to television, Nintendo, war toys, loud music, and other kinds of excitement. As they get older, they ride in fast cars, or experiment with alcohol, drugs, sexuality, or other things that tax their bodies and minds. We adults too try to fill our loneliness with these kinds of things, and all of us suffer. We have to teach ourselves and our children how to appreciate the simple joys that are available. This may not be easy in our complex, distracted society, but it is essential for our survival. Sitting on the grass with your little boy or girl, point out the tiny yellow and blue flowers that grow among the grasses and contemplate these miracles together. Peace education begins on this occasion.

CHAPTER EIGHT

Diet for a Mindful Society

*T*o realize peace in our daily lives, we need some guidelines. Two thousand five hundred years ago, the Buddha offered five wonderful precepts to Anathapindika and his friends as a practice to help them live a peaceful and wholesome life. Since that time in many Asian countries, these guidelines have served as the ethical basis of a happy life. I would like to present them to you in a way that makes their applicability clear for our situation today. Violence, racial injustice, alcoholism, sexual abuse, environmental exploitation, and so many other problems compel us to find ways to stop the suffering that is rampant in ourselves and in society. I hope you will reflect on these five precepts and try to practice them, either in this form or in the way they are presented in your own tradition.

The First Precept

Aware of the suffering caused by the destruction of life, I vow to cultivate compassion and learn ways to protect the lives of people, animals, and plants. I am determined not to kill, not to let others kill, and not to condone any act of killing in the world, in my thinking and in my way of life.

The foundation of all precepts is mindfulness. With mindfulness, we see that lives everywhere are being destroyed, and we vow to cultivate compassion as a source of energy for the protection of people, animals, plants, and our entire planet. Just feeling compassion is not enough. We also have to develop understanding so we know what kind of action to take. We must make the effort to stop all wars.

The mind is the basis of our actions. To kill with the mind is more dangerous than to kill with the body. When you believe that you have the only way and that everyone who does not follow your way is your enemy, millions may be killed. So it is not just by killing with our hands that we break the first precept. If, in our thinking and our way of life, we allow killing to go on, this is also an offense. We must look deeply. When we buy something or consume something, we may be participating in an act of killing. This precept reflects our determination not to kill, either directly or indirectly, and also to prevent others from killing. Vowing to practice this precept, we commit ourselves to protecting our planet and becoming bodhisattvas energized to practice love and compassion.

The Second Precept

Aware of the suffering caused by exploitation, social injustice, stealing, and oppression, I vow to cultivate loving kindness and learn the ways of working for the well-being of people, animals, and plants. I vow to practice generosity by sharing my time, energy, and material resources with those who are in real need. I am determined not to steal and not to possess anything that should belong to others. I will respect the property of others, but I will prevent others from profiting from human suffering or the suffering of other species on Earth.

Stealing comes in many forms. Oppression is one form of stealing, and it causes much suffering both here and in the Third World. Countries are torn by poverty and oppression. We want to help hungry children help themselves, for example, but we are caught in a way of life that keeps us so busy that we do not have time. We do not need a lot of money to help them. Sometimes they only need one pill or one bowl of food, but because we cannot free ourselves from our own small problems and our lifestyles, we don't do anything.

This precept is also about awareness of suffering and cultivating loving kindness. We may have the capacity of being generous, but we must also develop specific ways to express our generosity. Time is more than money. Time is for bringing joy and happiness to other people and thus to ourselves. There are three kinds of gifts—the gift of material resources, the gift of helping people rely on themselves, and the gift of non-fear. Helping people not be destroyed by fear is the greatest gift of all. This precept teaches us the very deep practice of sharing time, energy, and material resources with those who are in real need and truly reflects the bodhisattva ideal of compassion.

The Third Precept
Aware of the suffering caused by sexual misconduct, I vow to cultivate responsibility and learn ways to protect the safety and integrity of individuals, couples, families, and society. I am determined not to engage in sexual relations without love and a long-term commitment. To preserve the happiness of myself and others, I am determined to respect my commitments and the commitments of others. I will do everything in my power to protect children from sexual abuse and to prevent couples and families from being broken by sexual misconduct.

We practice this precept to help ourselves and others avoid being wounded, and to restore peace and stability in ourselves, our families, and society. A sexual relationship is an act of communion that should be performed in mindfulness, with love, care, and respect. "Love" is a beautiful word, and we have to restore its meaning. When we say, "I love hamburgers," we spoil the word. We have to make the effort to heal words by using them properly and carefully. True love includes a sense of responsibility and accepting the other person as he or she is, with all strengths and weaknesses. If you like only the best things in a person, that is not love. You have to accept his or her weaknesses and bring your patience, understanding, and energy to help the person transform. This kind of love is safe.

We use the phrase "love sickness" to describe the kind of love that makes us sick. It is a kind of attachment, or addiction. Like a drug, it makes us feel wonderful, but once we are addicted, we cannot have peace. We cannot study, work, or sleep. We think only about the other person. This kind of love is possessive, even totalitarian. We want to own the object of our love, and we don't want anyone to prevent us from possessing him or her totally. It creates a kind of prison for our beloved one. He or she is deprived of the right to be himself or herself.

The feeling of loneliness is universal in our society, and it can push us into a relationship. We believe naïvely that having a sexual relationship will make us feel less lonely. But when there is no real communication between you and the other person, a sexual relationship will only widen the gap and cause both of you to suffer.

The phrase "long-term commitment" is not strong enough to express the depth of our love, but we need to say something so people will understand. To love our child deeply, we have to make a long-term commitment and help him or her through the journey of life as long as we are alive. When we have a good friend, we also make a long-term commitment. How much more so the person with whom we want to share our body and soul. It is important to make such a commitment in the context of a community—family or friends—to witness and support you. The feeling between the two of you may not be enough to sustain your happiness in times of adversity. Even if you do not accept the institution of marriage, it is still important to express your commitment in the presence of friends who love and support you. It will give you peace, stability, and a greater chance for real happiness.

This precept also applies to society. There are many ways our families and society are destroyed by sexual misconduct. Many people suffer every day because they were molested as children. When you practice this precept, you vow to protect children and also those who sexually abuse children. The ones who cause suffering must also become the objects of your love and protection. They are the product of an unstable society, and they need our help. Our society needs bodhisattvas who practice in this field to prevent suffering and the breaking up of relationships, families, and individual lives.

The Fourth Precept
Aware of the suffering caused by unmindful speech and the inability to listen to others, I vow to cultivate loving speech and deep listening in order to bring joy and happiness to others and relieve others of their suffering. Knowing that words can create happiness or suffering, I vow to learn to speak truthfully, with words that inspire self-confidence, joy, and hope. I am determined not to spread news that I do not know to be certain and not to criticize or condemn things of which I am not sure. I will refrain from uttering words that can cause division or discord, or that can

cause the family or the community to break. I will make all
efforts to reconcile and resolve all conflicts, however small.
Loving speech is an act of generosity. When we are
motivated by loving kindness, we can bring happiness to many others through our kind words. When
we have a lot of pain, it is difficult to speak lovingly,
so it is important to look deeply into the nature of
our anger, despair, and suffering in order to be free of
it. If we use words that inspire self-confidence and
trust, especially with our children, they will flower.

In my tradition, whenever we want to inspire ourselves to practice the art of deep listening, we recite
this verse:

> We invoke your name, Avalokitesvara. We aspire
> to learn your way of listening in order to help
> relieve the suffering in the world. You know
> how to listen in order to understand. We invoke
> your name in order to practice listening with
> all our attention and openheartedness. We will
> sit and listen without any prejudice. We will sit
> and listen without judging or reacting. We will
> sit and listen in order to understand. We will sit
> and listen so attentively that we will be able to
> hear what the other person is saying and also
> what is being left unsaid. We know that just by
> listening deeply, we already alleviate a great
> deal of pain and suffering in the other person.

Deep listening is the basis for reconciliation. To
reconcile means to bring peace and happiness to

members of our family, society, and other nations. To
promote the work of reconciliation, we have to refrain from aligning ourselves with one party or another so that we understand both. This work takes
courage; we may be suppressed or even killed by
those we wish to help. After listening to both sides,
we can tell each side of the suffering of the other.
This alone will bring about greater understanding.
People are sorely needed to do this in many places in
the world, including South Africa, Eastern Europe,
the Middle East, and Southeast Asia. Our society
needs bodhisattvas who can bridge the huge gaps between religions, races, and peoples.

The Fifth Precept

*Aware of the suffering caused by unmindful consumption,
I vow to cultivate good health, both physical and mental,
for myself, my family, and my society by practicing mindful eating, drinking, and consuming. I vow to ingest only
items that preserve peace, well-being, and joy in my body,
in my consciousness, and in the collective body and consciousness of my family and society. I am determined not
to use alcohol or any other intoxicant or to ingest foods or
other items that contain toxins, such as certain TV programs, magazines, books, films, and conversations. I am
aware that to damage my body or my consciousness with
these poisons is to betray my ancestors, my parents, my
society, and future generations. I will work to transform
violence, fear, anger, and confusion in myself and in society by practicing a diet for myself and for society. I under-*

*stand that a proper diet is crucial for self-transformation
and for the transformation of society.*

In the West, people have the impression that their
body belongs to them, that they can do anything they
want to their body. They feel they have the right to
live their lives however they please. And the law
supports them. This is individualism. But according
to the teaching of interbeing, your body is not yours
alone. Your body belongs to your ancestors, your parents, and future generations, and it also belongs to
society and all other living beings. All of them have
come together to bring about the presence of this
body. Keeping your body healthy is an expression of
gratitude to the whole cosmos—the trees, the clouds,
everything. You practice this precept for everyone. If
you are healthy, physically and mentally, all of us
will benefit. We are what we consume and metabo-
lize. We have to eat, drink, and consume, but unless
we do it mindfully, we may destroy our bodies and
our consciousness, expressing a lack of gratitude to
our ancestors, parents, and future generations. Mindful consuming is the main subject of this precept.

It is important for each family to have at least one
meal together every day. This meal should be an occasion to practice mindfulness, and to be aware of
how fortunate we are to be together. After we sit
down, we look at each person and, breathing in and
out, smile to him or her for a few seconds. This practice can produce a miracle. It can make you real, and
it can make the others at the table real also.

Then we practice meditation on the food. One person looks at one dish on the table and describes its content and history. Children and adults can learn from this and have a deeper look into the nature of the food. This may take only a few minutes, but it will help everyone enjoy the food much more. For example, someone says aloud, "This bread, made from wheat, Earth, sun, and rain, comes to us after much hard work. The wheat was grown organically by a farmer in Texas, and a considerable amount of fuel was used to transport the flour to a conscientious bakery in our home town. May we live in a way that is worthy of this food, and appreciate the positive and negative elements that are present in each bite."

Eating in silence, even for a few minutes, is a very important practice. It takes away all the distractions that can keep us from really touching the food. Our mindfulness may be fragile and it may be too difficult to carry on a conversation and really honor the food at the same time. So for the first five or ten minutes, it is wonderful to eat in silence. In my monastic tradition, we practice the Five Contemplations before eating. The second Contemplation is, "We vow to be worthy of this food." I think the best way to make ourselves worthy of this food is to eat it mindfully. The whole cosmos has come together to make this food available, and someone has spent an hour or more preparing the food. It would be a pity if we didn't eat it in mindfulness.

After the period of quiet, we can practice mindful talking, the kind of talking that can increase the happiness in the family. We should never talk of things that can separate us; we should never reproach someone during the meal. That would spoil everything. Parents should refrain from discussing the mistakes their children have made, and young people should also only say things that will help bring about more happiness and nourish the mindfulness in the family, such as "Daddy, isn't this soup fantastic?" Speaking this way waters the seeds of happiness in the whole family. Life is an art. We should all be artists in order to live a happy life. We will have time later to discuss our business projects or what happened in school. During dinnertime we feel grateful that we are together, we have food to eat, and we really enjoy the food and the presence of each other.

It is important that we maintain a healthy diet. There are so many wonderful things to eat and drink; we have to refrain from consuming the things that harm us. Alcohol causes a lot of suffering. So many people have grown up receiving some form of abuse from an alcoholic parent. The fruit and grain that produce alcoholic beverages use farmland that could be producing food for those who are hungry. And so many traffic accidents involve someone who is intoxicated. When we understand that we are practicing not only for ourselves, we will stop drinking alcohol. To stop drinking is a statement to our children and our society that this is a substance not worthy of our support. Even if we don't drink alcohol, we may get killed by a drunken driver. In persuading one person to refrain from drinking, we make the world a safer

place. Drinking wine is an element running deep in
Western civilization, as is evident in the Eucharist
and the Sabbath meal. I have spoken with priests and
rabbis to see whether it might be possible to substi-
tute grape juice or some other beverage for the wine,
and they think it is possible.

Sometimes we don't need to consume as much as
we do. Consuming itself can become a kind of addiction, because we feel so lonely. Loneliness is one of
the afflictions of modern life. When we are lonely, we
ingest food in our body and into our consciousness
that can bring toxins into us. Just as we make every
effort to maintain a proper diet for our body, we must
also maintain a proper diet for our consciousness, refraining from ingesting toxic intellectual and spiritual
food. When we watch TV, read magazines or books,
or pick up the telephone, we only make our condition worse if our comsuming is not mindful. During
one hour watching a film filled with violence, we water the seeds of violence, hatred, and fear in us. We
do that, and we let our children do that. We need to
have family meetings to discuss an intelligent policy
for television watching. We may have to label our TV
sets the same way we label our cigarette packs:
"Warning: Watching TV can be hazardous to your
health." Children see so many violent images on television. We need an intelligent policy concerning the
use of television.

Of course there are many healthy and beautiful
programs, and we should arrange our time so that
the family will benefit from these. We don't have to

destroy our TV sets. We only have to use them with
mindfulness. We can ask television stations to broad-
cast healthier programs and encourage the boycott of
those who refuse. We can even support the manufac-
ture of TV sets that only receive signals from stations
that produce healthy, educational programs. We need
to be protected because the toxins are overwhelming,
and they are destroying our society, our families,
and us.

The idea of a diet is the essence of this precept.
Our collective consciousness has so much violence,
fear, craving, and hatred in it, and it manifests in
wars and bombs. Bombs are a product of the fear in
our collective consciousness. Just to remove the
bombs is not enough. Even if we were able to transport all the bombs to the moon, we would not be
safe, because the roots of the war and the bombs are
still in our collective consciousness. We will not abol-
ish war with angry demonstrations. We have to
transform the toxins in our own consciousness and in
our collective consciousness. We have to practice a
diet for ourselves, our families, and our society, and
we have to work with artists, writers, filmmakers,
lawyers, psychotherapists, and others if we want to
stop the kind of consuming that is poisoning our collective consciousness.

The problem is very big. It is not just a question of
enjoying one glass of wine. If you stop drinking alcohol altogether or stop watching unwholesome films
and TV programs, you do it for the whole society.
When you see that we are in great danger, refraining

from the first glass of wine is a manifestation of your enlightenment. You are setting an example for your children, your friends, and all of us. On French television, they say, *"Une verre, ça va, deux verres, bonjour les dégâts."* "One glass is all right, but two glasses are destructive." They don't say that if there were no first glass, there could not be a second.

Please join me in writing down three things. First, what kind of toxins do you already have in your body, and what kind of toxins do you already have in your psyche, your consciousness? What makes you suffer now? If you need to practice sitting or walking meditation in order to look deeply enough, please do so. When you have done this, please sit quietly for a few moments, and then look into the bodies and souls of your children, your spouse, or others who are close to you, since all of you are practicing together. Recognizing these toxins and listing them on a sheet of paper is meditation—looking deeply in order to call things by their true names.

Second, please ask yourself, "What kind of poisons am I putting into my body and my consciousness every day?" What am I ingesting every day that is toxic to my body and my consciousness? What is my family ingesting? What are my city and my nation ingesting concerning violence, hatred, and fear? The beating of Rodney King is a manifestation of how much hatred, fear, and violence are in our society. What kinds of poisons do we ingest every day in our families, our cities, and our nation? This is a collective meditation.

Third, write down a prescription that arises from your insight. For example, "I vow that from today I will not ingest more of this, this, and this. I vow only to use this, this, and this to nourish my body and my consciousness." This is the foundation of practice— the practice of loving kindness to yourself. You cannot love someone else unless you love and take care of yourself. Practicing in this way is to practice peace, love, and insight. When you look deeply, you have insight, and your insight brings about compassion.

Before you begin to eat, breathe in and out and look at the table to see what is good for your body and what is not. This is to practice the precept of protecting your body. When you want to watch TV or go to the movies, first look deeply in order to determine what should be viewed and what should not be viewed by you and your children. Think about the books and magazines you read, and decide what should be read and what should not be read by you and your children. Practicing together as a community, we don't need to take refuge in entertaining ourselves with any more poisons. Based on our own insight, we can decide what to ingest and what not to ingest into our bodies and our souls.

Please discuss with your family and friends a diet for your body, a diet for your consciousness, and also a diet for the collective consciousness of our society. This is a meditation practice, and it is true peace work. Peace begins with each of us taking care of our bodies and our minds every day.

I hope you will practice according to the letter and spirit of these five precepts, reciting them regularly, and discussing them with friends. If you prefer to use the equivalent from your own tradition, that is wonderful. At Plum Village, we recite these precepts every week. One person reads each precept slowly and then breathes three times before saying, "This is the (first) of the five precepts. Have you made an effort to study and to practice it during the last week?" We do not answer yes or no. We just breathe three times and let the question enter us. That is good enough. "Yes" would not be entirely correct, but "No" would not be correct either. No one can practice these precepts perfectly. If you are a vegetarian, for example, the food you eat still contains living beings. But we have to do something, and practicing the precepts is a direction we can follow to produce the dramatic changes that are needed in ourselves and in society.

Sangha Building

*E*very time I see someone without roots, I see him as a hungry ghost. In Buddhist mythology, the term "hungry ghost" is used to describe a wandering soul who is extremely hungry and thirsty but whose throat is too narrow for food or drink to pass through. On the full moon day of the seventh lunar month in Vietnam, we offer food and drink to the hungry ghosts. We know that it is difficult for them to receive our offerings, so we chant a *Mantra to Expand Hungry Ghosts' Throats*. There are so many hungry ghosts, and our houses are small, so we make these offerings in the front yard.

Hungry ghosts long to be loved, but no matter how much we love and care for them, they may not have the capacity to receive it. They may understand in principle that there is beauty in life, but they are not capable of touching it. Something seems to be standing in their way preventing them from touching these refreshing and healing elements of life. They want only to forget life, and so they turn to alcohol, drugs, or sex to help them forget. If we say, "Do not do that," they will not respond. They have heard enough admonitions. What they need is something to believe in, something that proves to them that life is meaningful. We all need something to believe in. To help a hungry ghost, we have to listen to him or her in mindfulness, provide him with an atmosphere of family and brotherhood, and then help him experience something good, beautiful, and true to believe in.

One afternoon in Plum Village, I saw a woman who looked exactly like a hungry ghost. Plum Village was beautiful at that time of year—the flowers were blooming and everyone was smiling—but she could not touch anything. I could feel her pain and suffering. She walked alone, and she seemed to be dying of loneliness with each step. She had come to Plum Village to be with others, but when she arrived, she was not able to be with anyone.

Our society produces millions of hungry ghosts, people of all ages—I have seen some not yet ten years old—who have no roots at all. They have never experienced happiness at home, and they have nothing to believe in or belong to. This is the main sickness of our time. With nothing to believe in, how can you survive? How can you find the energy to smile or to touch the linden tree or the beautiful sky? You are lost, and you live without any sense of responsibility. Alcohol and drugs are destroying your body.

Our government believes that the way to deal with the problem of drugs is to try to prevent drugs from being smuggled into the country and to arrest those who sell or use them. But the availability of drugs is only a secondary cause of the problem. The main cause is the lack of meaning in the lives of so many people, the lack of something to believe in. If you abuse drugs or alcohol, it is because you are not happy—you do not accept yourself, your family, your society, or your tradition, and you want to re-nounce them all.

We have to find ways to rebuild the foundations of our communities and to offer people something to believe in. The things you were offered in the past may have been too abstract and presented too coer-cively. Perhaps you thought that science would bring ease to society or Marxism would bring social justice, and your beliefs have been shattered. Even the God you prayed to—the one President Bush invoked to help the United States defeat Iraq—was too small. Many of the people who represented your traditions had not themselves experienced the deepest values of the tradition; they only spoke in its name and tried to force you to believe, and you felt turned off.

Mindfulness is something we can believe in. It is our capacity of being aware of what is going on in the present moment. To believe in mindfulness is safe, and not at all abstract. When we drink a glass of water and know that we are drinking a glass of wa-ter, mindfulness is there. When we sit, walk, stand, or breathe and know that we are sitting, walking, stand-ing, or breathing, we touch the seed of mindfulness in us, and after a few days, our mindfulness will grow quite strong. Mindfulness is the kind of light that shows us the way. It is the living buddha inside of each of us. Mindfulness gives birth to insight, awakening, compassion, and love.

Not only Buddhists, but also Christians, Jews, Muslims, and Marxists can accept that each of us has the capacity of being mindful, everyone has the seed of mindfulness in himself or herself. If we know how to water this seed, it will grow, and we will become alive again, capable of enjoying all the wonders of life. I know many families that were about to break, but whose harmony has been restored thanks to the practice of mindfulness. That is why if you ask me what I believe, I would say that I believe in mindfulness. Faith is the first of the five powers taught by the Buddha. The second is energy, the third mindfulness, the fourth concentration, and the fifth understanding. If you do not have faith, if you do not believe in anything, you are without energy. That is why faith brings about energy. A good friend is someone who can inspire faith.

When we touch the ground, we can feel the stability of the Earth. We can also feel stability in the sunshine, the air, and the trees—we can count on the sun to rise tomorrow and the trees to be there for us. We have to put our trust in what is stable. When we build a house, we build it on solid ground. When we say, "I take refuge in the sangha," it means we put our trust in a community of fellow practitioners who are solid. A teacher can be important and also the teachings, but friends are the most essential element of the practice. It is difficult or even impossible to practice without a sangha.

As we look deeply in order to discover our true self, we find that what we have been calling a "self" is made entirely of non-self elements. Our body and mind have their roots in society, in nature, and in those we love. Some of us may not like to talk or think about our roots because we have suffered so much from the violence of our family or our culture. We want to leave these things behind and search for something new. It is easy to understand why we feel this way, but when we practice looking deeply, we discover that our ancestors and our traditions are still in us. We may be angry at them, but they are still there, urging us to come back and connect with their joys and their pains. We have no choice but to get in touch with the roots that are in us. The moment we connect with them, a transformation takes place in us and our pain begins to melt away. We see that we are an element in a continuation of our ancestors, and we are also the way for future generations.

It is not possible for us to throw away one thing and run after another. Whether our tradition is Christianity, Judaism, Islam, or something else, we have to study the ways of our ancestors and find the best elements in the tradition for ourselves and our children. We have to live in a way that allows the ancestors in us to be liberated. The moment we can offer joy, peace, freedom, and harmony to our ancestors, we offer joy, peace, freedom, and harmony to ourselves, our children, and their children at the same time.

Many people were abused or beaten by their parents, and many more were severely criticized or rejected by them. Now in their store consciousness, these people have so many seeds of unhappiness they don't even want to hear their father's or their mother's name. When I meet someone like this, I always offer the meditation on the five-year-old child, which is a mindfulness massage. "Breathing in, I see myself as a five-year-old child. Breathing out, I smile to the five-year-old child in me." During the meditation, you try to see yourself as a five-year-old child. If you can look deeply at that child, you can see that you are vulnerable and can be easily hurt. A stern look or a shout can cause internal formations in your store consciousness. When your parents fight and scream at each other, your five-year-old receives many seeds of suffering. I have heard young people say, "The most precious gift my parents can give is their own happiness." By living unhappily, your father made you suffer a lot. Now you are visualizing yourself as a five-year-old child. When you smile at that child in yourself, you smile with compassion. "I was so young and tender, and I received so much pain."

The next day, I would advise you to practice, "Breathing in, I see my father as a five-year-old child. Breathing out, I smile to that child with compassion." We are not used to seeing our father as a five-year-old child. We think of him as having always been an adult—stern and with great authority. We have not taken the time to see our father as a tender, young

boy who can also be easily wounded by others. So
the practice is to visualize your father as a five-year-
old boy—fragile, vulnerable, and easily hurt. If it
helps, you can look in the family album to study the
image of your father as a boy. When you are able to
visualize him as vulnerable, you will realize that he
may have been the victim of his father. If he received
too many seeds of suffering from his father, of course
he will not know how to treat his son well. So he
made you suffer, and the circle of samsara continues.
If you don't practice mindfulness, you will do exactly
the same to your children. The moment you see your
father as a victim, compassion will be born in your
heart. When you smile to him with compassion, you
will begin to bring mindfulness and insight into your
pain. If you practice like that for several hours or several days, your anger toward him will dissolve. One
day, you will smile to your father in person and hug
him, saying, "I understand you, Dad. You suffered
very much during your childhood."

Through meditation, we rediscover the value of
our families and our roots, including those values
that have been buried under years of suffering. Every
tradition has some gems, the fruits of thousands of
years of practice. Now they have come down to us,
and we cannot ignore or deny them. Even the food
we eat has our ancestors and our cultural values in it.
How can we say that we have nothing to do with our
culture? We can find ways to honor our own tradition, and other traditions as well. Meditation teaches
us the way to remove barriers, limits, and discrimina-

tion in order to see the non-self elements within the self. Through the practice, we can remove the dangers of separation and create a world in which our children can have peace. Divisions between people, nations, and religious beliefs have contributed much to our suffering for many centuries. We have to practice in a way that releases these tensions in ourselves and between peoples so we can open up and enjoy one another as brothers and sisters. In whatever tradition you practice, if you obtain insight into the nature of interbeing, it is true meditation.

Some people, some hungry ghosts, have become so uprooted that we really cannot ask them to go back to their own roots, at least not yet. We have to help them by providing an alternative, a second chance. People like this live on the margin of society, and, like trees without roots, they cannot absorb nourishment. I have met meditators who have been practicing for twenty years who are still unable to transform themselves because they are so rootless. The practice is to help them get some roots, to find an environment where they can take root.

In Asia we have made an effort to model practice communities after families. We call one another dharma brothers, dharma sisters, dharma uncles, or dharma aunts, and we call our teacher a dharma father or mother. The children in Plum Village call me "Grandpa Teacher." I always approach them as a grandfather, not as someone outside the family. A practice center should possess that kind of warmth, that kind of familial brotherhood and sisterhood that will continue to nourish us. In the context of a spiritual family, we have a real opportunity, a second chance, to get rooted. The members of the sangha are aware that we are seeking love, and they treat us in a way that we will have the best chance to be rooted in this second family. They do their best to take care of us, acting like a sister or a brother to us. After three or six months, a smile is born on our lips when some real relationship between us and another member of the sangha is seen and acknowledged, and they know we are beginning to make progress and that transformation will be possible. New roots are beginning to spring out.

Interpersonal relationships are the key for success in the practice. Without an intimate, deep relationship with at least one person, transformation is unlikely. With the support of one person, you have stability and support, and later you can reach out to a third person, and eventually be a brother or sister to everyone in the sangha. You demonstrate your willingness and capacity to live in peace and harmony with everyone in the sangha.

It is my deep desire that communities of practice in the West be organized this way, as families in a friendly, warm atmosphere, so that people can succeed in their practice. A sangha in which each person is an island, not communicating with each other, is not helpful. It is just a collection of trees without roots. Transformation and healing cannot be obtained in such an atmosphere. We must be rooted if we want to have a chance to learn and practice meditation.

The nuclear family is a rather recent invention. Besides mother and father, there are just one or two children. Sometimes in such a small family, there is not enough air to breathe. When there is trouble between father and mother, the whole family feels the effects. The atmosphere in the house is heavy, and there is nowhere to escape. Sometimes the child may go to the bathroom and lock the door just to be alone, but there is still no escape; the heavy atmosphere permeates the bathroom, too. So the child grows up with many seeds of suffering and then transmits these seeds to his or her children.

In the old times, uncles, aunts, grandparents, and cousins all lived together. Houses were surrounded by trees where they could hang hammocks and organize picnics, and people did not have many of the problems we have now. When mother and father were having a problem, the children could always escape by going to an aunt or an uncle. They still had someone to look up to, and the atmosphere was not so threatening. I think that communities that practice mindful living can replace our former big families, because when we go to these communities, we see many aunts, uncles, and cousins who can help us.

Having a community where people gather as brothers and sisters in the dharma and where children have a number of uncles and aunts is a very wonderful thing. We have to learn to create that kind of family. We have to see the other members of the community as our brothers and sisters. This is already a tradition in the East, and it can be learned in the West. We can take the best from both cultures.

Here in the West, I have seen many single parents. A single parent can also benefit from a practice community. He or she may think that it is necessary to remarry to have more stability, but I do not agree. You may have more stability now by yourself than you did when you were with a partner. Another person coming into your life could destroy the stability you now have. It is most important to take refuge in yourself, recognizing the stability you already have. By doing so, you become even more solid, and you develop yourself into a refuge for your child and your friends. So first you have to make yourself into someone stable and give up the idea that you cannot be yourself unless "that someone" is with you. You yourself are sufficient. When you transform yourself into a comfortable hermitage, with air, light, and order inside, you begin to feel peace, joy, and happiness, and you begin to be someone others can rely on. Your child and your dharma brothers and sisters can all rely on you.

So first return to your hermitage and arrange things from within. You can benefit from the sunshine, the trees, and the Earth. You can open your windows for these healthy, stable elements to enter, and you become one with your environment. When unstable elements try to enter your hermitage, close the windows and do not let them in. When thunder, high winds, or great heat want to intrude, prevent them from entering. Being a refuge unto yourself is a basic practice. Do not rely on someone you do not know much about, someone who may be unstable. Go back to yourself and take refuge in your own hermitage.

If you are a mother raising your child alone, you must learn how to do it. You have to be a father also; otherwise you will continue to need someone else to play the role of a father for your child, and you will lose your sovereignty, you will lose your hermitage. If you can say, "I can learn how to be both a father and mother to my child. I can succeed by myself, with the support of my friends and my community," it is a good sign.

The love of a father is different from that of a mother. A mother's love is somehow unconditional. You are the child of your mother, that is why you are loved by her. There is no other reason. A mother tries to use her body and mind to protect that very soft, vulnerable part of herself. She has a tendency to consider her child as an extension of herself, as herself. This is good, but it may create problems in the future. She has to learn gradually that her son or daughter is a separate person.

A father's love is a little different. The father seems to say, "If you do this, you will receive my love. If you don't, you will not." It's a kind of deal. I have that in myself, too. I am capable of disciplining my students, and I also have the capacity of loving my students as a mother. I know it is not easy for a mother to be a father, but if you have a good sangha and good relationships with those in the sangha, other members of your sangha can be an uncle or an aunt for your child. With a community of practice, a single parent can be self-sufficient. She is capable of playing the roles of both mother and father, and she can also benefit from the help of some of the other adults.

Single parenting is widespread in the West. We need retreats and seminars to discuss the best ways to raise our children. We do not accept the ancient way of parenting. At the same time, we have not fully developed modern ways of parenting. We need to draw from our own experiences and practice and bring another dimension to the life of the nuclear family. When nuclear family life is combined with the life of a practice community, a sangha, it can be very successful. You can bring your child to the practice center very often, and both you and your child will benefit from the atmosphere there. The practice center will benefit from your presence also. Children are jewels who can help the practice. If the children are happy, all the parents and non-parents will enjoy the practice.

It is a joy to find ourselves in the midst of a sangha where people are practicing well together. Each person's way of walking, eating, and smiling can be a real help to us. She is walking for me, I am smiling for her, and we do it together, as a sangha. By practicing together like this, we can expect a real transformation within us. We don't have to practice intensively or force ourselves. We just have to allow ourselves to be in a good sangha where people are happy, living deeply each moment, and transformation will come naturally, without much effort.

I think that sangha building is the most important art for us to learn. Even if we are a skilled meditator and well versed in the sutras, if we don't know how to build a sangha, we cannot help others. We have to build a sangha that is happy, where communication is open. We have to take care of each person, staying aware of his pain, her difficulties, his aspirations, her fears and hopes in order to make him or her comfortable and happy. This requires time, energy, and concentration.

Each of us needs a sangha. If we don't have a good sangha yet, we should spend our time and energy building one. If you are a psychotherapist, a doctor, a social worker, a peace worker, or if you are working for the environment, you need a sangha. Without a sangha, you will not have enough support, and you will burn out very soon. A psychotherapist can choose among his or her clients who have overcome their difficulties, who recognize you as a friend, a brother, or a sister in order to form a group of people to practice as a sangha, to practice being together in peace and joy in a familial atmosphere. You need brothers and sisters in the practice in order to be nourished and supported. A sangha can help you in difficult moments. Your capacity of helping people can be seen by looking at those around you.

I have met psychotherapists who are not happy with their families, and I doubt very much that these therapists can help us if we need them. I proposed that they form a sangha. Among the members of this sangha are people who have profited and recovered from their illness and have become friends with the therapist. The sangha is to meet and practice together—breathing, living mindfully and in peace, joy, and loving kindness. That would be a source of support and comfort for the therapist. Not only do meditators and therapists have to learn the art of sangha building, every one of us needs to. I do not believe that you can go very far without a sangha. I am nourished by my sangha. Any achievement that can be seen in the sangha supports me and gives me more strength.

To build a sangha, begin by finding one friend who would like to join you in sitting or walking meditation, precept recitation, tea meditation, or a discussion. Eventually others will ask to join, and your small group can meet weekly or monthly at someone's home. Some sanghas even find land and move to the countryside to start a retreat center. Of course, your sangha also includes the trees, the birds, the meditation cushion, the bell, and even the air you breathe—all the things that support you in the practice. It is a rare opportunity to be with people who practice deeply together. The sangha is a gem.

The principle is to organize in the way that is most enjoyable for everyone. You will never find a perfect sangha. An imperfect sangha is good enough. Rather than complain too much about your sangha, do your best to transform yourself into a good element of the sangha. Accept the sangha and build on it. When you and your family practice doing things mindfully, you are a sangha. If you have a park near your home where you can take the children for walking meditation, the park is part of your sangha.

A sangha is also a community of resistance, resisting the speed, violence, and unwholesome ways of living that are prevalent in our society. Mindfulness is to protect ourselves and others. A good sangha can lead us in the direction of harmony and awareness.

The substance of the practice is most important. The forms can be adapted. During one retreat at Plum Village, a Catholic priest asked me, "Thây, I see the value of mindfulness practice. I have tasted the joy, peace, and happiness of it. I enjoy the bells, the tea meditations, the silent meals, and the walking. My question is, how shall I continue to practice when I get back to my church?"

I asked him, "Is there a bell in your church?"

He said, "Yes."

"Do you ring the bell?"

"Yes."

"Then please ring the bell the way we ring the bell here. In your church do you share a meal? Do you have tea or cookies?"

"Yes."

"Please do it the way we do here, in mindfulness. There is no problem at all."

When you go back to your own tradition, when you go back to your sangha or start a new sangha, you can enjoy doing everything you do in mindfulness. It is not necessary to throw away your tradition or your family. Keep everything and introduce mindfulness, peace, and joy into it. Your friends will see the value of the practice through you—not through what you say, but through your being.

CHAPTER TEN

Realizing Ultimate Reality

We come to the practice of meditation seeking relief from our suffering, and meditation can teach us how to transform our suffering and obtain basic relief. But the deepest kind of relief is the realization of *nirvana*. There are two dimensions to life, and we should be able to touch both. One is like a wave, and we call it the historical dimension. The other is like the water, and we call it the ultimate dimension, or nirvana. We usually touch just the wave, but when we discover how to touch the water, we receive the highest fruit that meditation can offer.

In the historical dimension, we have birth certificates and death certificates. The day your mother passes away, you suffer. If someone sits close to you and shows her concern, you feel some relief. You have her friendship, her support, her warm hand to hold. This is the world of waves. It is characterized by birth and death, ups and downs, being and nonbeing. A wave has a beginning and an end, but we cannot ascribe these characteristics to water. In the world of water, there is no birth or death, no being or non-being, no beginning or end. When we touch the water, we touch reality in its ultimate dimension and are liberated from all of these concepts.

The second century philosopher Nagarjuna asked, "Before something was born, did it exist or not?" Before the egg was born from a chicken, was it existent or nonexistent? If it were already there, how could it have been born? Since a baby is also already present in the womb of her mother, how can we say she is not yet born? Nagarjuna says that something already present cannot be born. To be born means from nothing you become something; from no one you become someone. But nothing can be born from nothing. A flower is born from soil, minerals, seeds, sunshine, rain, and many other things. Meditation reveals to us the no-birth of all things. Life is a continuation. Instead of singing "Happy Birthday," we can sing "Happy Continuation." Even the day of our mother's death is a day of continuation; she continues in many other forms.

A friend of mine has been taking care of her 93-year-old mother. The doctors say that her mother will die any day. For more than a year, my friend has been teaching her mother meditation exercises that have been very helpful. She began by watering the seeds of happiness in her mother, and now her mother becomes very alive every time my friend comes around. Recently she told her mother, "This body is not exactly yours. Your body is much larger. You have nine children, dozens of grandchildren, and also great-grandchildren. We are all continuations of you, and we are very happy and healthy. You are quite alive in us."

Her mother was able to see that, and she smiled. My friend continued, "When you were young, you were able to teach many people how to cook and do many other things. You made people happy. Now we are doing the same thing; we are continuing the work you have begun. When you were young, you wrote poetry and sang, and now many of us write poems and sing beautifully. You are continuing in us. You are many beings at the same time." This is a meditation on non-self. It helps her mother see that her body is just a small part of her true self. She understands that when her body departs, she will continue in many other forms.

Who can say that your mother has passed away? You cannot describe her as being or non-being, alive or dead, because these notions belong to the historical dimension. When you touch your mother in the ultimate dimension, you see that she is still with you. The same is true of a flower. A flower may pretend to be born, but it has always been there in other forms. Later it may pretend to die, but we should not be fooled. She is just playing a game of hide-and-seek. She reveals herself to us and then hides herself away. If we are attentive, we can touch her anytime we want. Your mother is also playing a game. She pretended to be born as your mother, she played the role of a mother so well, and then she pretended not to be there in order to help you grow up.

One day as I was about to step on a dry leaf, I saw the leaf in the ultimate dimension. I saw that it was not really dead, but it was merging with the moist soil and preparing to appear on the tree the following spring in another form. I smiled at the leaf and said, "You are pretending."

In the *Lotus Sutra*, the Buddha tells us about a physician who had many children. One time while the physician was away, his children ate something toxic and got food poisoning. When he returned home and saw them all sick, he gave them the proper medicine right away. Some of the children took it and got well, but others did not because they relied solely on the presence of their father. Finally the physician had to hide and pretend that he had died in order to get his children to take their medicine. Maybe your mother is playing that kind of game with you to encourage you to practice peace and happiness.

Everything is pretending to be born and pretending to die, including the leaf I almost stepped on. The Buddha said, "When conditions are sufficient, the body reveals itself, and we say the body is. When conditions are not sufficient, the body cannot be perceived by us, and we say the body is not." The day of our so-called death is a day of our continuation in many other forms. If you know how to touch your mother in the ultimate dimension, she will always be there with you. If you touch your hand, your face, or your hair, and look very deeply, you can see that she is there in you, smiling. This is a deep practice, and it is also the deepest kind of relief.

Nirvana means extinction, the extinction of all notions and concepts, including the concepts of birth, death, being, non-being, coming, and going. Nirvana is the ultimate dimension of life, a state of coolness, peace, and joy. It is not a state to be attained after you die. You can touch nirvana right now by breathing, walking, and drinking your tea in mindfulness. You have been "nirvanized" since the very non-beginning. Everything and everyone is dwelling in nirvana.

Nikos Kazantzakis tells the story of St. Francis of Assisi standing in front of an almond tree in midwinter. St. Francis asked the tree to tell him about God, and suddenly the tree began to blossom. In just a few seconds, the almond tree was covered with beautiful flowers. When I read this story, I was very impressed. I saw that St. Francis stood on the side of the ultimate dimension. It was winter; there were no leaves, flowers, or fruits, but he saw the flowers.

We may feel that we are incapable of touching the ultimate dimension, but that is not correct. We have done so already. The problem is how to do it more deeply and more frequently. The phrase, "Think globally," for example, is in the direction of touching the ultimate dimension. When we see things globally, we have more wisdom and we feel much better. We are not caught by small situations. When we see globally, we avoid many mistakes, and we have a more profound view of happiness and life.

There are times when we feel angry at someone, and we think that if we do not confront him, our dignity will be lost. Perhaps that person challenged our authority, and we feel frustrated that we did not respond right away. We may go to bed unhappy and barely manage to get a good night's sleep, but the next day, we feel completely different. We laugh and smile, and see the situation entirely differently. Suddenly, what happened yesterday is not important. Only one night separates us from the event, and already things are quite different. This is to think globally, in terms of time.

When we dwell in the historical dimension, we are tossed about by many waves. Perhaps we have a difficult time at work. Or we have to wait too long in line at the supermarket. Or we have a bad telephone connection with our friend. We feel tired, a little depressed, or angry. This is because we are caught in the present situation. But if we close our eyes and visualize the world one hundred years from now, we will see that these problems are not important. Embracing just one hundred years, we see things very differently. Imagine how drastic a change is brought about by touching the ultimate dimension!

We are entirely capable of touching the ultimate dimension. As I write this page, I am aware that my feet are on the ground in Plum Village, standing on French soil. I am also aware that France is linked to Germany, Spain, Czechoslovakia, and Russia, and even to India, China, and Vietnam. Thinking globally, I see that I am standing on more than just a spot, because when I touch Plum Village, I touch all of Europe and Asia. China is just an extension of the small piece of land under my feet. Standing on one part of the Eurasian continent, I am standing on the whole continent.

This kind of awareness transforms the spot you are standing on to include the whole Earth. When you practice walking meditation and realize that you are making steps on the beautiful planet Earth, you will see yourself and your walking quite differently, and you will be liberated from narrow views or boundaries. Each step you take, you see that you are touching the whole Earth. When you touch with that awareness, you liberate yourself from many afflictions and wrong views.

When you touch one thing with deep awareness, you touch everything. The same is true of time. When you touch one moment with deep awareness, you touch all moments. According to the *Avatamsaka Sutra*, if you live one moment deeply, that moment contains all the past and all the future in it. "The one contains the all." Touching the present moment does not mean getting rid of the past or the future. As you touch the present moment, you realize that the present is made of the past and is creating the future. Touching the present, you touch the past and the future at the same time. You touch globally the infinity of time, the ultimate dimension of reality. When you drink a cup of tea very deeply, you touch the present moment and you touch the whole of time. It is what St. Francis did when he touched the almond tree so profoundly that he could see it flowering even in the middle of winter. He transcended time.

Meditation is to live each moment of life deeply. Through meditation, we see that waves are made only of water, that the historical and the ultimate dimensions are one. Even while living in the world of waves, we touch the water, knowing that a wave is nothing but water. We suffer if we touch only the waves. But if we learn how to stay in touch with the water, we feel a great relief. Touching nirvana frees us from many worries. Things that upset us in the past are not that important, even one day later— imagine when we are able to touch infinite time and space.

We come to the practice seeking relief in the historical dimension. We calm our body and mind, and establish our stillness, our freshness, and our solidity. We practice loving kindness, concentration, and transforming our anger, and we feel some relief. But when we touch the ultimate dimension of reality, we get the deepest kind of relief. Each of us has the capacity to touch nirvana and be free from birth and death, one and many, coming and going.

Last autumn while in England, I had a dream that seemed epic in nature. My brother, An, and I were in an open marketplace when a man invited us to come look at a stand in the corner of the market. When we arrived there, I immediately recognized that every item on display represented an event that I had directly lived and experienced with my brother and those close to me. Almost all of the items, the experiences, were of suffering—poverty, fire, floods, storms, hunger, racial discrimination, ignorance, hatred, fear, despair, political oppression, injustice, war, death, and misery. As I touched each item, a feeling of sorrow arose in me, and also a feeling of compassion.

Then we walked into the center of the stand and stood beside a long table, on which were displayed many elementary school notebooks. At the left end of the table, I recognized one notebook as mine and one as my brother's. I approached my notebook and looked through its pages, and I recognized in it many happy and meaningful experiences I had had during my childhood, and also many experiences of suffering. Then I looked through my brother's notebook and recognized our experiences together as little boys. I have been writing the memoirs of my childhood, but I had not included any of the materials that were in those notebooks. Perhaps these were experiences I lived only in dreams and had forgotten when I woke up. Perhaps they were experiences from previous lives. I was not sure which, but I was certain that these experiences were authentically mine, and I had the idea to bring these materials home so I could include them in my memoirs. I was very pleased with this idea, as I didn't want to forget again.

At the very moment I had this thought, I heard the man who had invited us to come look at the stand pronounce a terrible sentence. Standing on my right, he said, "You will have to go through all of this again!" The way he spoke, it sounded like a verdict or a condemnation, and his voice conveyed that he had the authority to decide such a thing. He sounded like God, or Destiny. I was shocked! Do I really have to go through all that suffering again, all that fire, flood, storm, hunger, racial discrimination, ignorance, hatred, despair, fear, sorrow, political oppression, misery, war, and death? I had the feeling I had gone through these things for countless lifetimes, together with my brother and all my companions from the past. We had been through so many dark tunnels, and now we were finally in a place with space and freedom. Did we really have to go through these experiences again?

I felt a kind of revulsion, and I said to myself, "Oh no!" But in less than a second, my reaction changed. I pointed two fingers of my right hand into the man's face and told him with all my determination and might, "You cannot frighten me. Even if I have to go through all of this again, I will do it! Not just once, but thousands more times if that is necessary. And all of us will do it together!"

At that moment, I woke up and could not remember the contents of the dream. I only knew I had just had a powerful and important dream. So I stayed in bed and practiced conscious breathing, and slowly the details came back. I understood that the man represented something I had to find out, and my first thought was that I was going to die very soon in order to begin anew the journey that had been appointed to me. I felt calm. Dying was no problem for me at that time. I was not afraid. I told myself that the only thing to do was tell Sister True Emptiness, one of my closest companions over the past thirty years, so that she and others would be prepared. But right away, I could see that it was not true that I had to die at that moment. The dream had to have a deeper meaning.

Looking more deeply, I discovered that the man represented the seed of fear, or laziness, in me, the equivalent of Buddha's Mara, and it arose from the depth of my soul, my store consciousness. In my first reaction to him, I had been standing in the historical dimension, the dimension of the wave. But in my second reaction, I was acting from the ultimate dimension, the dimension of water. When I touched the world of no birth and no death, I was no longer afraid, and I demonstrated that by pointing my two fingers in his face. I saw that the strength that had helped me challenge the man was the energy of faith born from insight and freedom. I had told him in a lucid way that since insight and freedom were present, I had the strength and courage to go through any kind of hardship countless times.

I looked at my clock. It was 3:30 in the morning. I thought of the children in Vietnam, Cambodia, Somalia, Yugoslavia, and South America, and I felt a strong solidarity with all of them. I felt ready to go through these hardships with them, again and again. And then I saw you, my dear friends who have been practicing the Way of Emancipation. I saw that you are also ready to join us, so that together we can bring our collective wisdom and freedom to the chil-

dren of the world and help them bear these hardships.

When we studied the *Lotus Sutra* last year at Plum
Village, we discussed the ultimate dimension and the
historical dimension; and then we added the action
dimension, represented by bodhisattvas practicing
engaged Buddhism. Having touched the ultimate dimension, these bodhisattvas return to the historical
dimension to help however they can to transform the
suffering and offer relief. They live the life of a wave,
but they also live the life of water, and in doing so,
they offer us non-fear.

You, my brothers and sisters, my companions on
the Way, are those very bodhisattvas riding on the
waves of birth and death without drowning in birth
and death. We have gone though interminable suffering, an endless tunnel of sorrow and darkness. But
we have practiced, and through the practice we have
obtained some insight and freedom. Now it is time
for us to join with the children—the children of all
colors—and bring our strength to bear on the chal-
lenges that are before us. I am sure we will do better
this time.

Resources for the Practice

Plum Village is a community of practice located in southwestern France. The best time to visit is during the summer opening from July 15 to August 15, but any time of year is possible. Please write for information:

Plum Village
Meyrac
47120 Loubès-Bernac, France

The Community of Mindful Living organizes retreats; raises funds to help those in need, especially in Vietnam; and publishes *The Mindfulness Bell* newsletter. Each issue of the newsletter includes a dharma talk by Thich Nhat Hanh, other essays on the practice, a listing of local sanghas worldwide, accounts of daily practice experiences, and a current schedule of retreats and days of mindfulness. For further information or to subscribe to *The Mindfulness Bell* ($12 per year; $16 outside the U.S.), please write to:

Community of Mindful Living
P.O. Box 7355
Berkeley, California 94707

Parallax Press publishes books and tapes on socially engaged Buddhism, including all works in English by Thich Nhat Hanh. Please write for our free catalog:

Parallax Press
P.O. Box 7355
Berkeley, California 94707